'Mesmeric and dreamlike in the richness of its setting, *I am Henry* offers a new perspective on the story of Henry VIII from the vantage point of Limbo. It is an intensely satisfying – if at times unsettling - read, providing the meetings and encounters that you always wished had happened. *I am Henry* both re-evaluates a notorious life from a novel perspective, as well as taking his story forwards, beyond his death. A compelling read.'
Elizabeth Norton, Historian and Author

'We all want to know what would happen, and *I am Henry* has Henry VIII's spirit being confronted by Anne Boleyn, Catherine of Aragon and Henry, Duke of Cornwall, his short-lived son by Catherine, among others, and they're all keen to share their thoughts on him. The setting is atmospheric, and we have some wonderfully poignant and emotionally charged scenes as Henry has to re-evaluate his life and answer to others. Will he submit and repent and thereby gain eternal peace and salvation?'
Claire Ridgway, Historian and Author

'*I am Henry* is a highly imaginative and emotionally engaging story of repentance and redemption. It masterfully personifies the various characters and helps readers see them as fully realised people rather than mere faces in a painting, as we so often experience them. The story also offers some great insights into human nature, why we resist change, and the emotional journey that often leads to it. I see this finding a ready audience amongst the fans of the short film that inspired this novel. Not to mention those who are fascinated by Henry VIII and his wives.'
Kevin Miller, Author

I AM HENRY

An innovative retelling of the story of
Henry VIII and Anne Boleyn

Copyright © 2023 Jan Hendrik Verstraten
& Massimo Barbato
ISBN-13: 978-84-125953-4-5

M
MadeGlobal Publishing

For more information on
MadeGlobal Publishing, visit our website
www.madeglobal.com

Cover Design: Arash Jahani

To Francien and Lidia, the women who have shaped our lives.

TRUTH

CHAPTER ONE
LAST DAYS

THE LONG DESERTED CORRIDOR, with its smooth marble floor, stretches deep into the cold darkness of the night. Henry shivers. He is not in Whitehall anymore. This is Richmond Palace. His father's palace. The home of his youth.

He is seventeen years old again. With a racing heart, he makes his way toward the patches of light coming through the cracks of one of the doors at the end of the corridor.

He hesitates before he knocks on the door and then waits. There is no answer, but from inside his father's privy chamber, he hears a man's raw and distressed voice sobbing. The man cries out, pleading for more time and promising to be a better man. Alarmed, Henry opens the door, ready to enter his father's domain.

The frail, sickly old man is on his knees beside his bed. He is holding a wooden crucifix above his head. Full of fervour, he kisses the crucifix and then holds it in his arms as if cradling a newborn baby. He begs God for mercy while beating his chest.

"Papa," Henry whispers. He wants to go over and console him, but something holds him back. He knows it is not only death that his father fears but also the dread of judgment from Almighty God.

"*Circumdederunt me gemitus mortis, dolores inferni circumdederunt me,*" the late king prays. "The sorrows of death have assailed me. The pains of hell have encompassed me."

Troubled to see his father consumed by so much angst and inner turmoil, Henry now wishes he had not intruded, but just when he is about to leave his father in peace, the floorboards under his feet creak. Startled, his father looks up at him, his eyes filled with tears and despair.

"I shouldn't have come here," Henry says, but it is too late.

As if paralysed, Henry opens his eyes and gasps in horror. It is no longer his father's presence that frightens him. A tall, dark shadow approaches him. Henry can feel the figure's breath on his skin and smell the foul odour of his rotting teeth.

"Death," Henry mutters. He tries to lift his arms to protect himself but then realises it is his good friend Denny who is leaning over him, his face close to Henry's.

"Your Majesty," Denny whispers, resting his hand on Henry's shoulder. "You're not expected to live much longer, and if I may say so, Your Highness, you should repent of your sins. This is something every good Christian must do in the hour of their death."

Henry lets out a wail of anguish before he can speak. "You sound worried," he says, trying to smile, but Denny is right, of course. "Christ in all His mercy will pardon me of my sins. I truly believe so."

"Should I send for an educated man to whom you can confess your sins?" Denny asks.

Henry has thought of this as well. "If I have to choose someone," he replies, pausing to catch his breath, "it should be the archbishop, of course, Dr Cranmer."

Henry feels blessed to have Denny by his side. A tall, athletic man, he is a beacon of strength and devotion to his king. Henry trusts him completely. It was the right decision to give him the honourable task of the groom of the stool. Denny is discreet and witty, with an uncanny ability to make Henry laugh even in the most unpleasant circumstances. It is prudent that Denny is part of his innermost circle and a prominent member of the privy chamber.

Denny is also rightly in charge of the "dry stamp" of the king's signature. It is remarkable how ordinary and unnoticeable he appears at court, despite his influential position and the wealth that comes with it. That speaks volumes about the humble and earnest man that Denny is.

"Should I send for the archbishop now?" Denny asks, but this can wait. It is better to get some sleep first.

Henry's decline began weeks earlier with severe aches and pains, frequent fevers and vivid hallucinations. Confined to his bed, the sweat and stench of decay became part of his sorry existence. It enraged him at first, and when he complained in those early days to Denny or the queen, he was like an erupting volcano, full of self-pity. Now he has come to terms with his wretched state. Surrendering to it has brought him some peace and given him patches of time to reflect, in some strange way allowing him to explain himself to an invisible audience.

"Nothing in my life is private or personal," he growls. "It's all political. Who I sleep with, how my health is, whom I allow to live or condemn to die. Everything I do or don't do is a matter of the state and has far-reaching consequences. To understand me, if you care to do so, is to grasp this simple fact. I am the law, and the fate of the country and its subjects rests entirely upon my shoulders."

Looking back, he struggles to focus on the matter of his own importance. He has had this problem for a long time now. Ever since he fell off his horse, it feels as if his mind finds it difficult to finish sentences or to bring a series of thoughts to a conclusion. The truth is his heart is empty. Void of emotion. A dungeon with many dark chambers and chains.

This is a bitter realisation for a man who used to possess an abundance of passion about life, nature and everything, a romantic who dreamed bigger dreams than anyone else. He saw the beauty in people once. Some would call him sentimental, and maybe he was at times. In his own eyes, he always saw himself as a prince with a big heart and a loving spirit.

For him to have become king was not merely his lot or privilege. It had been a destiny bestowed on him by God and God alone. A heavy burden to carry indeed. Often a terribly lonely path as well, but did it not say in Proverbs, *'The king's heart is in the hand of the Lord, like the rivers of water; He turns it wherever He wishes'*?

He lies in bed and lets out a deep sigh, bringing his hand to his large stomach. The pain has subsided. Only random memories remain, and fruitless efforts come with it to piece it all back together.

It was after his elder brother, Arthur, died that Henry's fate was sealed. To be the royal heir and future king became his sole focus. It added gravitas to his life and a fair amount of excitement and pleasure. Of course, he was still young and fortified with physical strength, charm and ideals in those early years. He was admired and cheered on by his peers. The memory humours him. He had to fight hard to be without an equal. He clenches his fist as if he still fights for victory. In the end, he always succeeded. He smiles. No one could compare to him.

Dark thoughts enter his mind. He was crushed and chastened far too soon, as all men are in life. He tries to push such thoughts away. They remind him of his impotence as a man, a father and a king. The disaster struck when his firstborn son, Henry, Duke of Cornwall, died seven weeks after his birth.

A sudden sharp pain fills his chest. He gasps for air. "Oh my God, have mercy," he whispers. He takes it as a warning that he should not think about these things. This was all such a long time ago. Other matters of state are more important now.

Do not be mistaken; long before he ordered his chief minister that it was forbidden to mention his deteriorating health and impending death, he said, "I know that traitors lie in wait, ready to take the throne away from me and my dearest son and heir, Edward, Prince of Wales. There are a great many Judases at court, and they can be found among the best and closest of friends. Believe me, I know."

When his waist inflated to fifty-four inches and his leg was covered with ulcers, he realised the end was near. He was plagued by gout and struggled to walk and breathe. They had to carry him around in a wooden chair and help him sit and turn over in bed.

These were testing times for certain, but the nights were the worst. The worry of how to prepare for what was to come kept him awake. As resilient and shrewd as he is, he never exhibited any weakness to those around him, though privately, he agonised about how it would be in those final moments. Would the right prayers be said afterwards for the salvation of his soul?

CHAPTER TWO
THE KING IS DEAD

IT IS EARLY MORNING at Whitehall Palace. The heavy, sumptuous curtains in his bedchamber are drawn, and the rich tapestries, religious paintings and luxurious rugs adorning the chamber are mostly hidden in the dark. The dim light from the tapers in the silver candelabras provides him with a measure of comfort and protection from the harsh winter outside, and he takes pleasure in how the flames cast strange shadows on the walls and ceiling.

His head rests upon several soft pillows whilst his enormous frame lies underneath a blanket on a four-poster bed covered with ornate carvings and dressed with a canopy of crimson velvet drapes. Years of excessive living and merrymaking have taken their toll on his body, but he is not in too much pain. Not anymore. His leg, which has troubled him so much over the years, no longer feels like it is part of him.

The servants take good care of him. He does not doubt their loyalty and devotion, but his perception of the world around him has altered over the last twenty-four hours. Sometimes he recognises those who attend to him, but there are instances when their presence is sketchier, as if the room is filled with fog. He can hear their voices, but the words sound muffled and disjointed, as though he is underwater.

It irritates him not to understand what is going on. With anguish, he grunts and snorts from time to time like a wounded boar. They rush to his bedside and, with hushed voices, ask him endless questions. They plump up his pillows and straighten the bedcovers. To his embarrassment, he lies exposed to their inquiring eyes and exploring hands.

Despite frequent efforts to feed him a flavourless broth, he has not eaten for days. The herbal remedies, a concoction consisting of sage, lavender, marjoram and chamomile, do little to cure his nausea or ease the pressure that stretches across his chest.

Throughout the night, he feels disoriented. He knows his time is near, but somehow it does not worry him anymore.

At one point, a ghostly apparition appears to him—his mother. Rather than be alarmed, he is soothed by her gentle voice as she calls his name.

"Henry, my son, we're all here waiting for you." She smiles, and he reaches out to touch her. The intimacy of the moment brings tears of joy to his eyes. He takes a long, strained breath.

"Mother…" His voice is soft and frail. Then, in a blink of an eye, and in the most natural way imaginable, he finds himself standing beside his bed rather than lying on it. His mother, on the other hand, is nowhere to be seen.

Curious, Henry moves closer to study his large body, which is still lying there. Every breath his body takes is laboured and accompanied by a rattle.

A moment later, the door to his bedchamber opens. Thomas Cranmer enters, dressed in a clerical vest and black Canterbury cap. The portly man observes the large body in the bed with concern. Henry smiles when he sees him. He has always enjoyed the archbishop's intellect and reassuring nature.

"I fear the time is near," Denny tells Cranmer.

The archbishop sits next to the bed. As Henry watches events unfold, he tries to catch Cranmer's attention, to no avail. Focused on the matter at hand, the archbishop leans forward, sighing deeply, and grabs hold of the king's hand. Henry's fingers and palm are swollen and lifeless. His gold rings and encrusted rubies are a stark contrast to the softness of his pale, mottled skin.

Denny stands at the foot of the bed and looks with anticipation for Cranmer's next move. As Henry observes his good old friend, Denny appears tired and depressed. The last several months, filled with restrictions and distress, have taken their toll on him.

Henry's eyes suddenly begin to flicker. His breathing becomes shallow and then, without warning, stops altogether. Unsettled by this, Cranmer leans over the body to investigate. Raw, guttural noises are emitted from Henry's throat. His chest convulses and contracts for one last time before his entire body freezes. Henry observes it all from the edge of the bed, detached and unafraid. Cranmer and Denny are fixated on the lifeless body in the bed, waiting for any signs of life. A minute goes by, then another, but there is only silence.

Cranmer turns to Denny, nods to confirm what they both suspect, and then releases the king's hand from his grip.

"His Majesty, King Henry the Eighth, by the Grace of God, the King of England, France and Ireland, is dead. Let us pray for the repose of his soul," Cranmer declares, then marks the king's forehead with the sign of the cross.

"Yes, of course," Denny murmurs, then hesitates, still in shock. In unison, they recite the Lord's prayer.

Henry notices Denny's tears. Is he weeping for him? A feeling of warmth overcomes Henry, and he reaches out to his friend to comfort him. But the moment he approaches him, Denny starts to tremble and lets out a deep sigh. Henry pulls back, afraid his proximity as an unearthly being may have frightened his friend.

"His Majesty will be missed," Denny says. He looks at Cranmer, who remains silent and self-contained.

Later that day, other members of the privy chamber arrive to pay their final respects to the king. There is Edward, of course, Henry's nine-year-old son and heir, a clever and inquisitive young man with a great motivation to learn and form his own opinions. The young prince sits beside the bed. Behind him stands his uncle, Edward Seymour, Lord Protector of England and the first Duke of Somerset. Like Henry, the prince has fiery-red hair and fine facial features. A white feather adorns his black hat, and a gold chain is draped across his ermine-furred overcoat and silk vest. In many ways, Edward is a mini version of Henry himself, though he lacks his father's natural charisma. He appears fragile and in a state of shock.

Denny, who knows the boy and his uncle well, addresses them both, explaining in detail what occurred earlier that day. Still affected by it all, Denny needs to pause at times to regain his composure.

"The last time the king spoke, he asked for Dr Cranmer. He was quite weak, and he commanded me to send for him. Not much later, he stopped speaking altogether, and I was not even sure he was still with us." Denny turns toward Cranmer, who takes it from there.

"After I arrived and spoke to him," Cranmer begins, "His Majesty reached for my hand. I sat down next to him. He held my hand tightly but did not utter a word. I urged him to put his trust in Christ and to call upon His mercy, and I told him, though he could not speak, to give a signal with his eyes or with his hand that he trusted in the Lord. The king squeezed my hand as hard as he could. Shortly afterwards, he departed this world."

The following morning, a servant draws open the bedchamber's curtains, flooding the room with daylight for the first time in weeks. Nonetheless, the pungent smell of death lingers in the air. The king's lifeless body is laid out on the bed, dressed in formal attire to resemble the monarch he once was.

His daughters, Lady Mary and Lady Elizabeth, enter the bedchamber. Both princesses wear black, as is customary.

Mary, who is thirty years old, looks composed but removed in her demeanour. Her hair is hidden beneath a gable headdress worn over a coif. Henry likes to believe he had an amicable relationship with Mary. Despite this, he often felt burdened by her presence. Some told him that they thought she was sweet and loyal to those close to her but that she had a nervous and restless temperament and was difficult to fathom.

How different he felt in Elizabeth's presence. His thirteen-year-old daughter could be too spirited at times, and he often had to reprimand her, but in truth, he thought she carried a deep love in her, and he regretted that she appeared lonely at court. When he asked others about their impressions, they all reassured him that she was fun-loving and strong.

At his deathbed, Elizabeth is visibly depressed and ill at ease. Her long red hair hangs loosely over her shoulders. She starts to cry when she sees her father's corpse. She is now an orphan, as are all of his children.

Catherine Parr, the queen dowager, his rock in those final days, is dressed in mourning and sits beside his bed. The large black jet stone ring with its striking image of a skull worn on her finger was made especially for this occasion.

Henry observes the women with a mixture of curiosity and sadness. The queen greets Mary and Elizabeth, but it is conspicuous how withdrawn and reticent she is. She does not converse with either of them. Elizabeth, on the other hand, sobs without end. Neither of the older women attempts to comfort the child, and Henry longs to soothe his youngest daughter's sorrow. Suddenly, Elizabeth looks up and stares in his direction. Does she see him?

CHAPTER THREE
SYON

A MURDER OF CROWS takes flight that morning, cawing
above the solemn cortège as it departs Whitehall Palace. The
procession is a grand spectacle as it meanders through the bleak,
wintry landscape.

Henry's leaden casket is carried on a chariot drawn by black-
caparisoned horses. The servants of the royal household are dressed
in mourning. They walk alongside the carriage in silence while
banners surrounding the cortège portray the saints and the Virgin
Mary, just as Henry wanted.

Roads along the route have been cleared of snow and even
widened for the occasion. Priests greet the cortège as it passes by
their churches, and bishops stationed by the roadside offer masses
for the repose of his soul.

At one point, Henry stands behind a clergyman alongside the
road who, when the cortège passes, sprinkles it with holy water
and honours it with incense. Henry is pleased to witness it all,
except for the absence of spectators. Where are the crowds of
loyal subjects to bid him farewell? Why is there no spontaneous
outpouring of grief?

At dusk, the cortège draws near Syon Abbey, where it is
scheduled to stop for the night. The abbey is located on the
meadows between Syon House and the Thames, across the river
from the palace at Richmond.

Light from the abbey is seen in the distance and brings sighs
of relief from weary members of the party. Henry observes their

arrival from the abbey's steps. He is all too familiar with the great abbey's history before the Reformation. Surrounded by ornate cloisters and tall outbuildings, Syon's once unique influence and importance as a place of scholarship was unquestionable.

The route taken did not come as a surprise to Henry. He spent many days planning the funeral with Denny and the queen. It was important to him that it all be carried out in detail, as he wished.

Upon arrival, the Bishop of London, whom Henry knows well, greets the cortège with Edward Seymour. Seymour, always a meddler, delivers instructions to the captain. Moments later, the captain signals the sixteen-strong yeomen of the guard to lift the weighty casket from the carriage. They carry it up the narrow steps leading into the abbey.

As the bells ring to mark their arrival, the party of servants and guests disperse and follow the casket into the building, where a chorus of evening vespers emanates from the chapel. Tomorrow, the cortège will continue its journey toward Windsor as planned. It will be where the funeral will take place.

A beam of moonlight penetrates a stained-glass window, which lights up one half of a vast underground crypt while the other side remains in total darkness. A wooden partition painted in gold divides the hall in two at the far end.

A frightened mouse squeaks and scuttles across the floor of the crypt. Henry snaps out of his absent-mindedness. He hesitates as if trying to make sense of what has happened, and for the first time since his death, he explores his new ethereal body.

He pinches his waist and arms to discover an athletic physique in its prime and one very much alive, at least to him. This feels odd after months of sickness. He touches his groomed beard and his face for confirmation. His skin is smooth and not wrinkled, as it was at the end of his life.

He notices the rings on his fingers and feels the impressive dark sable and gold chain around his shoulders. All these earthbound symbols of wealth and status feel familiar and exciting.

With pleasure, he tilts his head up and, using both hands, rearranges his hat. Then he plants his right fist proudly on his thigh and poses. He smiles as he recalls when he instructed Hans Holbein the Younger to paint him this way on a large mural in the presence chamber next to his throne.

In the painting, he dominates the scene, which depicts him as a powerful, larger-than-life king standing beside his beloved wife, Jane. The reactions to the mural from those granted an audience always pleased him.

As he crosses the floor and heads toward the partition, the clopping sound of his leather boots echoes in the crypt.

In the centre of the enclosed sanctuary stands the enormous casket that carries his corpse. A single candelabra lights the dark space. Its candles flicker and emit a soft light whilst an odour of frankincense disguises the pungent smell of rotting flesh.

Behind the coffin in the semi-darkness of an alcove, a Bridgettine monk sits and meditates in silence. Henry assumes he has been there for quite some time. The monk is covered by the large hood of his black habit. Only his pale lips are visible.

His presence surprises Henry at first. The crypt is part of Syon Abbey, once the Bridgettine order's home, before the break with Rome. The community had long since fled in exile, so inviting a Bridgettine to sit with the royal casket seems a controversial and misguided choice.

Despite this, Henry does not question the monk's presence and no longer considers the Reformation the important matter it once was when he was alive. As Henry stands at the foot of the casket, he is irked by the overweight wax effigy adorning it. Why did they make him look so grotesque?

Suddenly, the monk stirs from his seat and gets up. He stands still for a moment as if in deep thought and then brushes past Henry as though he is unaware of him. This may be a good moment to stop the man and ask him questions or give orders, but Henry's mind goes blank, and, like a prisoner who has lost his free will, he follows the monk in the dark without resistance.

CHAPTER FOUR
THE TRIAL

TOGETHER THEY CROSS the large main hall and enter a gate that leads toward a tenebrous room. A hubbub of chattering voices can be heard coming from inside. The noise gets louder as they approach. It is a large gathering of people, probably awaiting Henry's arrival.

Inside, Henry finds the room to be large. It resembles an ecclesiastical courtroom, dimly lit, with tall iron candle holders positioned in each of the room's four corners.

It is packed with rows of unfamiliar spectators sitting on hard wooden benches. No one turns around when he enters or pays him their respects. This is all very strange for someone like Henry, who is used to being the centre of attention.

Still, he recognises he is not his usual self, and this is not a normal situation. It is like being in a dream, although not a regular one. His surroundings are as vivid and real as anything in life can be.

The monk takes a seat in the back, out of sight. Henry, on the other hand, walks with confidence farther along the main aisle to get a better view of the proceedings. He spots an empty seat in the front row and sits down. Intrigued, he takes a moment to look around.

In the sparse light, the faces in the crowd appear hostile, like a mob that has come to see a villain punished for his crimes. Who are these wretched people? Why do they gather here in the middle of the night?

A bishop he doesn't recognise is seated on a pulpit. Situated close by is a witness stand, behind which a slender woman wearing a long black velvet cape waits. Her face is hidden beneath the hood of her cape, but her graceful figure is surrounded by an ethereal light which captivates everyone, Henry included.

When she removes the cape and turns to face the mob, the chatter in the room falls silent. The woman who stands before the court looks proud and self-assured. She is Anne Boleyn.

His second wife looks as radiant and as regal as ever. She is wearing an exquisite gold satin and velvet gown, and her dark hair is loose around her shoulders. An ornate gold chain with a diamond pendant is draped around her neck. It is difficult not to be taken in by her beauty and charm once more. As he stares at her, he holds his breath.

Anne always had an alluring quality that drew much attention and admiration from both sexes. And, as always, she stands there as if she belongs — in the centre of things, with all eyes on her. Vulnerable yet strong, she exudes grace, but it is neither her beauty nor how she conducts herself that Henry thinks about.

She has been dead for twelve years. It feels like an eternity. Even so, he remains haunted by the memory of her treason: the adultery and the horrifying charges of incest with her brother and detailed accounts from first-hand witnesses. If there is anyone he does not want to see, it is her.

Anne looks around the crowd confidently before she turns to the bishop, who gets up from his seat.

"Your Grace," the bishop begins, introducing the proceedings, "this is a preliminary hearing to present the charges against your former husband, King Henry the Eighth. You've been invited here as a witness to share your testimony. The court desires to review His Majesty's life and investigate if he deserves to be pardoned for his sins. The verdict and sentencing will take place at a later date, and judges will be appointed in due course. Until such time the defendant will be held in Limbo."

The crowd murmurs. What sins is he referring to? What did he mean by a verdict and sentencing, and where is this place called "Limbo" he speaks of?

The bishop addresses Anne. "We hope you can shed some light on your relationship with His Majesty. Please start from the beginning."

"My Lord, how does one describe being asked to become queen, only to discover that one is merely a pawn on the king's chessboard? A pawn he will sacrifice without hesitation or scruples when it suits him? You may wonder why I, an educated woman, fell into his trap. Why did I not recognise his callous and immoral character before it was too late? Why did I agree to love him?"

Anne pauses for a moment as if wondering how it all came about. "The truth is not flattering, but I worshipped and adored him as my king when we met. I admired him as the talented musician and poet, the relentless sportsman and the skilled hunter I accompanied on many occasions. He was a man among men, and I believed he was greater than any of them. My desire has always been to love and to be loved, truly and without any reserve."

The bishop leans forward and stares at her. "Was it your intention to seduce the king and make him fall in love with you despite his marriage to Her Majesty, Queen Catherine of Aragon?"

The court is quiet, the people staring at Anne in anticipation of a salacious response. Her character and moral standing are at stake. She has been branded an adulteress, an evil woman and a pariah. With the evidence stacked against her, how will she defend her honour?

"I didn't plot to win his affections," she replies. "On the contrary, I initially feared him more than I loved him. I was all too aware that when he declared to me that he was stricken with the dart of love, this dart could easily be forged into a dagger or a sword."

Henry listens to her testimony with aversion. Some of what Anne says may be true, but what does the truth matter if the person who delivers it is a liar?

"But His Majesty grew fond of you?" the bishop asks.

"Yes. He wanted me. He was unstoppable. You have to understand he was a powerful man. He was the king. He could choose whomever he wanted, and he chose me." Anne pauses for a moment. "It was me he wanted. No one else."

"Traitor!" Henry shouts out from the aisle. The crowd is shocked by his sudden outburst.

"Murderer!" Someone in the crowd yells across to Henry. Other derogatory names immediately follow like sharp arrows aimed solely at him. He cannot dodge the mob's tirade of abuse, which is ugly to witness. How could such a thing be permitted?

"Order, order!" the bishop shouts, trying to restore calm. The mob listens, but Henry ignores the bishop and loses control. He can no longer contain the anger boiling inside of him.

"She betrayed me," he scoffs, pointing his finger at Anne.

The audience breaks out in another uproar. Anne grins at Henry in satisfaction as if she has just emerged the victor in battle.

"Order!" the bishop cries out again, and the crowd simmers down.

"Your Grace, there are no further questions," he says, indicating that Anne is dismissed. She gives the mob a coquettish smile, then steps down from the stand and, without looking back, picks up her cape and leaves the courtroom by a side exit.

Henry, meanwhile, struggles to keep his composure. There is so much more he needs to say, not only to the court but also to her. But the nightmarish spectacle does not end there.

A grand lady who died long ago enters the court and takes her place at the stand. The effect on the audience is enormous, and the crowd gasps and gawps in awe at her presence.

CHAPTER FIVE
REVELATIONS

SHE RESEMBLES A MATRIARCH. She could even be a
saint, Henry thinks. After all, it is Catherine of Aragon, Queen
of England, daughter of King Ferdinand II of Aragon and Queen
Isabella of Castile, who is about to give her testimony.

Henry is mesmerised by his first wife's presence. He can't
take his eyes off her. In the candlelight, her skin is flawless and
surprisingly untarnished by age.

His attention is drawn to the large mother-of-pearl-encrusted
cross around her neck. It complements her gable hood and
sumptuous gown, also in gold and black, although it's a more
conservative style than Anne's.

He suddenly feels weak and light-headed. What on earth will she
say after all these years? He must try to pull himself together.

"Your Highness, the court finds it a great honour to welcome
you," the bishop says. "It values and acknowledges your years of
devoted service to the Crown as a queen, a wife and a mother. We
honour you for your loyalty to God Almighty Himself."

Catherine nods in approval. Knowing his ex-wife as well as
Henry does, he realises she appreciates the dignified introduction.
She was raised a proud Spanish princess who values formality and
tradition.

"We encourage you to tell us the truth about your marriage to
the king."

"Certainly," Catherine replies with her distinctive Spanish
accent. Henry watches with indignation. Following Anne's

testimony, he anticipates an even stronger desire for revenge.

"I knew it long before he knew it himself," Catherine begins with confidence. "I saw them dance and laugh together. The king gambled that he could do whatever he pleased, that he had no duties as a husband, and was free of guilt." Catherine looks determined. She is a woman who is certain of her cause. Henry fidgets in his seat with discomfort.

"Guilt, however, is a tough negotiator. It's like your shadow, following you wherever you go. You cannot separate yourself from it unless you avoid the light and spend your life in darkness, and that's exactly what he did. The moment he thought he had made a deal with his guilt and had come to an agreement, life itself negated its terms. His redemption never came." She pauses briefly. "It was only two weeks after my death that he fell off his horse. Fourteen days only. He was unconscious for two hours, and he was never the same man again. His leg never healed, and ulcers grew out of his flesh. That was his guilt that came out of his body. It made him deeply suffer. God bless his Soul. *Requiescat* in pace." Catherine makes the sign of the cross. The action annoys Henry. His ex-wife is a convincing player.

"Your Highness, we thank you for your testimony," the bishop says. "Is there anything else you would like to highlight or share about your life with the king? Anything that you feel we ought to know?"

Catherine takes her time before she replies. Henry imagines that her response will be the final dagger in his back. He has listened to her as one who listens to a troubled family member, overcome with pity and self-righteousness. He looks around the courtroom to see how the mob will respond. Those who are present are silent, waiting in anticipation to hear her tale.

"Throughout our marriage, there were strong eastern winds. The River Thames froze every winter, and the chill in the air was harsh and bitter," Catherine says. "I was pregnant six times but lost five of our babies. Three of them were boys, all named Henry. I called them our little angels and prayed daily for their souls."

Some of the spectators express their sympathy with a tut or a gasp. Her words move even Henry as he remembers the sadness of each of those tragic events. He wouldn't be human if he didn't show some degree of compassion.

"My chaplain told me that our Lord must have loved our babies too much for them to be in this cruel world," Catherine says, then looks up toward heaven. She rests her right hand on her heart as she pauses for breath.

"Nonsense," Henry says, feeling it's time to speak his peace. "It wasn't because of that." His heart hardens as he interrupts her train of thought. "If a man shall take his brother's wife, it's an unclean thing. They shall be childless."

Henry's bitter response shocks the mob. Even Catherine looks wounded and perplexed.

"You loved me. I know that," she says with a sincere voice, looking at him with penetrating blue eyes.

Henry recalls how he explained the reason for their divorce to her in the court at Blackfriars in 1529. His friends told him afterwards that he had done so with clarity and eloquence. For him, it was a deeply unpleasant experience.

Catherine would not sit still while he spoke and showed impatience and disrespect toward the proceedings and himself. When it was finally her turn to speak, she made no sense at all. She portrayed herself as a victim, just as she is doing now, a foreigner who had never been accepted by her new country.

She even dared to drag the memory of his own dear father into the proceedings. She claimed the late king had given his blessing to the marriage. Then she walked off, angry and defiant. It was a blank refusal to discuss the matter further, ignoring his orders — stubborn woman.

A young red-haired man steps forward to take up a position beside Catherine. Henry has never seen him before. He is about six feet tall and looks handsome in his olive-green silk over-gown with full upper sleeves, black hose and leather breeches.

"Who are you?" the bishop asks.

"Your Honour, I'm Henry, Duke of Cornwall. I was born on New Year's Day, 1511, and died the following month. I am His Majesty's first-born son." The young man presents himself with sincerity, which provokes sympathy from the mob. Henry studies the lad.

"I've come here to support my mother," he says. He looks at Catherine, who gives her son a loving smile.

"They're all here with us. All five of them," Catherine says, then holds out her hand to beckon the others to join them from the opposite aisle. Two boys in their early teens, dressed smartly, and two younger girls of about eight and eleven in pretty high-necked smocks join Catherine.

"Each of us honours you as our king and our father," the young Duke of Cornwall says while looking Henry in the eye. "We love and accept you as him to whom we owe our short-lived lives."

Henry gets up and moves toward the children to get a closer look. Their hair and features resemble his and their mother's. It is an exciting thought. He turns to the eldest. "You look healthy and strong. You all do." For a moment, his eyes fill up with tears. The duke extends his arms to him.

"My dear father, please take our love, and find your peace."

Overwhelmed by the young man's gesture, Henry wants to walk over to his son and hold him. He desires this more than anything, and also to receive the love and affection of all his children. But a sudden thought puts an end to it all.

"What kind of trickery is this?" he asks, pulling back. He looks around at the silent mob. "Who are you?" he shouts. "Are you here to judge me? Your king?"

Angry and upset, he turns away from Catherine and the children and storms out of the courtroom, disappearing into the darkness of the crypt.

Like a hunted fox, he hides in the stillness and obscurity of the sanctuary and nestles against a pillar on the floor, confused and uneasy about it all.

He realises this whole charade about the divorce was his fault for not standing up to Catherine during the final years of their marriage. She had a hold over him. It made him pity her. In return, she humiliated him in public, and she still does. It embarrasses him even though he knows he has to let it be.

The monk's footsteps approach him and stop nearby. When Henry turns his head toward him, Henry's eyes focus on the man's toes, poking out from underneath his habit. Henry looks up at him. This monk is not an ordinary monk. How could he be? Nothing is as it used to be.

"I know who you are and why you're here," Henry says in a depressed voice. "My time's up, isn't it?" The question is rhetorical. He knows his fate.

The man's face is in darkness, but it does not matter. Henry is not one bit curious about him. What he struggles to come to terms with is that it is all over. His life. His reign as king. His journey was long, and he had chances to be great, but did he take them? He is insecure about his legacy and feels he has achieved so little.

"I once hoped to be the monarch my brother was meant to be: a new King Arthur of our modern Tudor times," he says with regret. "But God decided against it."

CHAPTER SIX
THE VISITOR

THERE WAS AN INSTANCE during a hunt in Hertfordshire. It was late September, one of those early autumn days that still carry the sunny optimism of summer and yet bring the melancholy of the end of last season's rule. Henry steered his horse away from the others and found himself alone in the forest.

He was on the lookout for a deer he knew was close by. Without making a sound, he stood still and listened. As he waited for the deer to give itself away, the sun came out, and its glittering rays broke through the thick foliage of the forest. A strange sensation overwhelmed Henry as though the world was opening up to something much greater than himself and this reality. It was something incomprehensible to him, and yet very powerful, peaceful and real. Was it an encounter with God?

Henry sits alone on one of the pews positioned here and there along the crypt's interior walls. His recollection of the hunt cheers him, but his train of thought is broken by the sound of bells that flood the abbey above. He makes a mental note of the number of strikes: one, two, three in total.

It remains dark outside, and a single candelabra lights the area. Anne stands in the shadows and watches him like a lioness about to go in for the kill.

To attract his attention, she starts to hum the chorus of a song she learnt during her time in France. Anne was once admired for her singing talent. Henry immediately recognises her distinct vibrato. He loved it once.

"Anne... is that you?" he asks, surprised.

"Someone important must have died," she says, stepping into the light. "Your Majesty." She smiles furtively at him and bows her head. Her presence so soon after her testimony at the trial against him fills him with torrid emotions.

She walks over to the iron gate opposite him, places her hands on the frame, and then turns to look at him. "Don't tell me you still long for me," she says.

She enjoys teasing him. He is sure she is doing it to provoke him, but he decides to take the bait. Her remark makes him laugh, and he shakes his head in amusement. "For many years, your beautiful image tormented me day and night," he says with a self-satisfying smirk. "We men are such weak creatures."

Anne seems to enjoy his answer and plays with him some more. "It's within our biology as women to seduce, charm and dazzle you men so we can mould and control you." Her behaviour is flirtatious. He falls silent as he reminisces about their early days together. Perhaps this is her intention.

His amorous interest in her started at court but was interrupted by the horrible sweating sickness that swept through the country. It forced them apart for over a year. Anne had to go into quarantine at Hever, the Boleyn family residence, while he isolated himself at various other places in the country. During this period of separation, his desire for her grew so strong that it was almost unbearable. He sent her many gifts and asked her to become his official mistress. Anne returned everything and refused in no uncertain terms to become his lover. Much to his distress, she did not clarify how she felt about him and remained ambiguous in her intentions. This was absolute torture for him.

His initial infatuation turned into what could be called an obsession. He can see that now. It made him insecure and restless and kept him awake at night. He wrote to her repeatedly, expressing his deep feelings, hoping he would get a passionate response or any indication that she felt as he did. He needed reassurance that she could not imagine a life without him either. As always, he would sign off with, "Written by the hand of that secretary, who in heart, body and will is your loyal and most assured servant, Henry R." Then one day, unexpectedly, confirmation of her love for him arrived.

He looks at Anne in earnest. "That afternoon, I received your gift while you were away... the jewel that depicts a woman on a ship in a storm-tossed sea. I wept like a little boy. I was overcome with joy and happiness." It is a confession of sorts to underline how deeply he felt at the time.

"You understood its deep significance," Anne says with a faraway look in her eyes.

The thought of the gift still touches him. The jewel she sent him after his many pleas was a token that she must have thought about in great detail. It was imaginative and, more importantly, a declaration of her love for him. It was not a simple "yes", though. It was also a riddle and a vow that their love could be fulfilled and consummated—if the right circumstances and conditions were met. She meant marriage, of course. It was strange, as even though he knew this was impossible, it aroused him enormously.

Henry gets up and walks over to her. They look each other in the eye with an intensity only lovers share. Without thinking about it, he places his hand on her shoulder. The intimacy reflects the same emotions he once felt for her. She feels it, too; he can tell. There is a moment when it all comes back. Their love. Their desire.

"So, why did you desert me?" Anne asks angrily. There is pain in her eyes. Then her face hardens, and she frees herself from his hold as though she cannot bear him being near her. "I always obeyed you and did as I was told, even when it went against my deepest wishes and my own happiness."

"There was ample proof that you committed treason," he replies, feigning nonchalance as though stating a simple fact.

Cromwell, his chief minister, had warned Henry that he was in great danger and, as a good servant, asked his permission to appoint investigators to get to the bottom of the rumours. There was the suggestion that the queen's need for male attention went beyond innocent flirtation and included the mortal sin of adultery. If this were indeed the case, the charge would be treason. Those were dark days. Cromwell's words crushed Henry even though he already suspected it himself. He had been too afraid to ask his minister. It was as if Cromwell could read his mind.

As a consequence, Henry signed the required documents and gave Cromwell his approval to do whatever he felt was expedient to protect His Majesty's honour and the kingdom itself.

When private conversations between Anne and Mark Smeaton were observed and reported to Cromwell, Smeaton was arrested, interrogated and put under house arrest.

The charges laid against Anne were serious, but when Henry was informed of her illicit affair with the musician, it was the final straw. Far from being a nobleman, Smeaton was a servant, an inferior. It was an insult not only to Henry's standing as a husband but also to the Crown itself.

The events coincided with another important decision he had to make: the great matter of his succession. Unlike his contemporaries, King Francis I and Emperor Charles V, who had several healthy children, Henry was without a male heir and his dynasty was not secure. He was left with three options. First, he could marry off his ten-year-old daughter, Princess Mary, and hope for a grandson, which was not a reliable strategy. Second, he could make his bastard son, Henry Fitzroy, legitimate, and he had already taken some significant steps toward that. Third, he could get a new wife.

On May 2, Anne was charged with adultery with three men. Cromwell provided evidence that could not be disputed or explained away. It devastated Henry, but it was clear that harsh, swift action was required to root out this evil.

Even now, Henry is aware that Anne still ignores her betrayal as if it were a lie. Is she not interested in the truth? Who else but herself could she blame for her downfall? Henry? Her most devoted husband? He can see on her face that this is what she believes.

"Because of you, our daughter has grown up without her mother. What man rewards his wife's loyalty in such a brutal and sadistic way?" Anne asks, her eyes full of fire. She never backed down from a fight, even with him.

Henry moves closer behind her. He grabs her arm and pulls her toward him. She refuses to look at him.

"Nothing in my life is private or personal," he says with impatience. "I am the law. I thought you understood."

The church bells strike a quarter past the hour. Anne uses the interruption to break free from his grip.

"Your time has run out," she says with sarcasm. "Who would have thought this moment would come?"

He shakes his head in denial. She thinks she can control his emotions, but he won't let her.

"The hour of one's death is the time for truth, reflection and repentance," she continues, walking away from him and the gate.

Henry frowns. She is being ridiculous and talks nonsense. "If I were truly dead, I wouldn't be here, talking to you," he replies. "I would be with my dearest Jane, who granted me a son and an heir." This is a clever response designed to hurt her. She deserves it, and he is pleased with himself.

"Maybe this is your purgatory," she replies. When she turns around and looks at him, she has a mysterious smile, as though she has foresight into events to come. It provokes him. She is deliberately frustrating him and deserves to be put in her place.

"Jane was my one and only love, and when I die, I will lie beside her," he says. This is true, and she will have to accept it.

CHAPTER SEVEN
SACRIFICIAL LAMB

ANNE STANDS ten feet away from Henry with her back toward him. She looks pale, petite and vulnerable.

"In the darkest hour of my suffering in the Tower the night before my execution," she says with a voice full of emotion, "I remembered the words of Jesus, our Lord, on the cross. '*Eli, Eli, lama sabachthani?*' 'My God, My God, why have You forsaken Me?'"

While she speaks, he feels a pang of regret. "It was my duty to carry out the law," he replies.

They told him afterwards that she was composed when they arrested her and behaved like a queen even though she was taken to the Tower. It was not until she arrived inside the Tower and was greeted by the constable that she lost her courage. The presence of Sir William Kingston and the grim surroundings of the Tower came as a terrible shock, and at that moment, she must have realised what was happening. It was irreversible, final, futile.

"Clearly, no one who relies on the law is justified before God," she says, "because the righteous will live by faith and faith alone." Anne trembles when she says this. Her righteous anger catches him off guard, though the fact that she quotes Roman 1:17 amuses him, and he shakes his head in disbelief.

"Why did I ever fall in love with you?" he wonders aloud.

"At the time, I was engaged to Henry Percy," she replies with a rueful voice, "the most loyal and gentle man there is."

Henry was never bothered by Percy. Anne's closeness to the poet, Sir Thomas Wyatt, disturbed him more than her broken engagement with the rather pitiful Earl of Northumberland.

"When you arrived at court that first time and I saw you standing there, everything and everyone disappeared in front of me," he says with emotion. "You had this light around you. You were full of wit and confidence and surrounded by laughter and admiration."

Anne nods in remembrance. "I was terrified." She tries to restrain her laughter, but she can't resist.

"Never in my entire life had I felt so excited about a woman," he says. "You had all this banter and bravado. I desperately wanted you." He looks at Anne. He knows how to charm a woman.

Anne's guard is down. She smiles and seems to enjoy his flattery. "I know you did," she says. "Everybody did. It changed everything."

"I can still feel it now," he says. "You made me feel like a man." His passion for her is rekindled and rises to the surface. He walks over to her, takes her hands in his, and kisses her.

For a moment, they are locked together in a passionate kiss. She surrenders to it before pulling away from him. The expression on her face changes into one of horror and despair.

"On that fateful day, when I was taken to the Tower, I was certain I had gone mad. I knew it couldn't be true, but it was." She turns away from him to face the iron gate once more. "I asked Sir William Kingston if I was to die without justice."

"Even the poorest of the king's subjects are given justice," Henry replies. "I've always been a just and honourable king."

Anne does not seem to hear him; either that or she chooses to ignore him. She is in her own world now, and her words are no longer directed at him. Instead, she relives this terrible memory.

"I asked him if I should go into a dungeon. He shook his head. 'No, Madam,' he said. 'You shall go into your lodging that you lay in at your coronation.'"

Anne catches her breath before she continues. "In the following hours, I was shaking heavily and felt sick to my stomach. Repeatedly, I was overcome with spells of dizziness followed by a cold sweat. It made me shiver as if the hands of death itself had already entered my surroundings." All the colour in her face has disappeared.

"That night, I sat down with the gentlemen of my privy chamber," Henry says, "and arranged what needed to be done to protect our country and its king. Serious matters of state were raised, and I felt an apprehension about the days to come. Mostly, I felt happy and liberated."

"The chaplain accompanied me throughout that lonely night," Anne says as she grabs the iron gate with her fist and stares, distraught, into the darkness of the crypt. "Together, we prayed and asked the angels to prepare for my arrival and to protect my dear sweet Elizabeth.

"When I finally walked into the open court the next morning toward my death, I was struck by the sun's radiance, which blinded me. It was as if the gates of heaven had prematurely opened to welcome me. It gave me strength and certainty regarding my final destination.

"The crowd that had gathered fell silent when I approached the scaffold draped in black. Master Kingston helped me up the steps, reassuring me that it would be without pain and that I would have time to make a speech.

"When I stood on the scaffold and looked at the crowd in front of me, I recognised some of the faces. They stared at me in silence and disbelief. The atmosphere was charged. I was shaking and confused but tried to be calm and strong to say my words.

"'Good Christian people,' I said, 'I haven't come here to preach a sermon; I've come here to die, for according to the law and by the law, I'm judged to die. Therefore, I'll speak nothing against it.'"

Henry knows Anne's execution speech well. He was in London, planning for the days ahead. They read Anne's speech to him afterwards. He never forgot it. To hear her speak it aloud reminds him of it, and he mutters what she said on the scaffold to himself. "I'm come hither to accuse no man nor to speak of that whereof I'm accused and condemned to die, but I pray that God would save the king and send him long to reign over you, for neither a gentler nor a more merciful prince was there ever, and to me he was ever a good, a gentle and sovereign lord."

To speak her words touches his soul. Affected by her speech, tears stream down his face.

Anne finishes her speech: "'And if any person will meddle in my cause, I require them to judge the best. And thus, I take my leave of the world and of you all, and I heartily desire you all to pray for me. O Lord, have mercy on me. To God, I commend my soul. To Jesus Christ, I commend my soul. Lord Jesu, receive my soul."

Now, for the first time, he allows himself to feel the loss of their love. But when he looks at the gate, she is no longer in the crypt with him. Distraught, he stares at the emptiness in front of him.

Sometime later, he finds himself in front of one of the abbey's stained-glass windows, immersed in the scene of Jesus crucified on the cross. The depiction looks real to Henry and takes on a deeper meaning. A beam of moonlight penetrates it, bringing the scene's muted colours to life and revealing its full splendour.

The monk joins him at the foot of the window. Henry turns to him and recalls the familiar character from Dante Alighieri's magnificent poem, "The Divine Comedy." "Are you my Virgil, who will guide me to heaven?" he asks with a hint of irony. The monk does not answer him but gestures for Henry to follow him. It is time to leave the confines of the crypt once and for all.

CHAPTER EIGHT
THE DUKE'S PLAN

UPON HER ARRIVAL in the afterlife, Catherine found in her faith the inspiration and the foundation for a new existence. The heavenly realms and all the dimensions in between were open to her, but she discovered they are not governed by the same laws as on Earth. Time has no meaning here, and each departed soul has greater influence over their surroundings and events than one could imagine.

Like a miracle, one's inner-most thoughts carry the power to manifest a desire into reality. Good and happy thoughts thus can create joyful experiences, while the dark conflicted pondering of sinners can lead to nightmares of the worst kind.

She took up residence in a beautiful rustic castle reminiscent of her childhood home in Spain. Her parents, who had crossed over long before she did, welcomed her into the fold, along with the children she had lost. It was a joyful reunion, and her soul found immense happiness in raising her babies. She called them her "little angels" and discovered a contentment she never knew existed.

Her family, the House of Trastámara, was the most influential on the continent of Europe. Her sister, Isabella, was the Queen of Portugal; her sister, Joanne, the Queen of Castile and Aragon, and her nephew was none other than Charles V, the Holy Roman Emperor. Her parents were more commonly known as "*Los Reyes Catolicos*," the Catholic monarchs, and all the family members were pious devotees of the Church in Rome. She took pride in her heritage and insisted that a portrait gallery of all her relatives, both living and deceased, take centre stage in the large entrance hall of her heavenly castle. But apart from this indulgence, the interior is understated and sparsely decorated, with little value placed on luxuries.

In her private quarters, an altar adorned with marble cherubs is her favourite place to sit and pray. Portraits of her children at various ages hang on the walls. Only Young Henry and Mary, her two eldest, are shown as young adults. Notably, there is no portrait of their father anywhere to be seen. From Catherine's point of view, this is her sanctuary, her domain, and he has no place in it.

She was not surprised by Henry's sudden outburst at the hearing. She already knew him to be lonely, a pathetic husband needing constant attention and reassurance from others to make his life work. A stubborn and difficult man, Henry deserved his reputation later in life for being a tyrant and an unjust ruler. He is a doomed soul in her eyes, without hope or any prospect for salvation. The gates of heaven will not be open to him. How could they be? And that, she decides, is a good thing, the consequence of his choices.

Catherine kneels before the altar in her private quarters. She is dressed in a white silk gown with a bodice intricately beaded with mother of pearl. Her long red hair hangs freely over her shoulders, which softens her appearance.

She carries a rosary in her hand made from rosewood that emits a strong, sweet scent. Catherine takes one of the beads and squeezes it hard. Then she focuses her attention on a beautiful statue of the Madonna.

"*Ave Maria, gratia plena, Dominus tecum. Benedicta tu in mulieribus, et benedictus fructus ventris tui, Jesu…*"

The light from the nearby candelabra flickers upon her cheeks, and her blue eyes sparkle like sapphires. As she continues to recite the Rosary, she tries to imagine the Lord being tried by the Sanhedrin and before Pontius Pilate, but she can only picture Henry's face.

"*Mater Dei, ora pro nobis peccatoribus, nunc, et in hora mortis nostrae. Amen.*" She makes the sign of the cross and slowly rises from the floor. Standing before the altar, she bows in reverence and then walks away.

Those last years of her life were years of hardship. She could never have imagined the humiliation she would encounter when she first arrived on England's shores. Back then, she was a young and naïve fifteen-year-old girl destined to marry Henry's older brother, Arthur. When he died soon after their marriage, she did everything to serve Henry and his country. He was a few years younger than her, and she used this to her advantage.

As regent, when Henry was away, she even won a decisive war against James IV and his Scottish troops for him. Her courage was a valuable asset to Henry's reign.

To end up a pariah banished from the royal court who would spend the rest of her days in cold, damp and inhospitable residences without staff or visitors was a deliberate move on his part to make her disappear without killing her. Her family was too powerful for him to put her on the scaffold, so he made her a prisoner in her own home.

He was a monster who even forbade her to see their daughter, Mary. Catherine understood why. Her husband was terrified of an uprising or a foreign plot to restore the dominance of the Catholic Church.

Her dearest son Henry, Duke of Cornwall, stands in front of her. She adores his visits and smiles as he curtsies before her. He was the first of her angels to greet her after she died, which made her truly happy.

She was surprised he was not a baby anymore but glad he had turned into such a fine and honourable young man. Any mother would be proud. Catherine extends her hands to him. He takes them and kisses them.

"I was right about your father, wasn't I?" she says. Before he answers, Young Henry looks away, aware that what he is about to say will concern her and cause a great deal of angst.

"For a brief moment, I saw love in his eyes."

Catherine looks at her son, dumbfounded. She gestures for him to sit next to her. "Come, my angel. Tell me what preoccupies your mind," she says.

"I want to help him. My father." He looks at her as if he has already made a plan.

It does not take her long to dismiss such a silly idea. "I forbid it," she insists. Catherine does not expect him to question her authority in the matter, but he is not one to give up easily. They are similar in that regard.

"Let me talk to him once more. Please, Mother. Trust me on this."

She shakes her head and becomes agitated. "He had his chance. You reached out to him, but he rejected you. He rejected all of us." Catherine recalls the devastation she felt in the courtroom.

"Please listen to me," he implores, but she interrupts him before he can finish.

"Your father doesn't pray. As with everything else, he wants someone else to do it for him. Do you truly think a man who doesn't pray can enter heaven?"

"I believe there is a way," he insists. "God's mercy extends even to the greatest of sinners if their heart is open to it." It was a clever answer for someone so young.

Catherine's demeanour begins to soften. No one is like her son. He is pure. Uncorrupted. A bundle of light and happiness. There is not a sinful bone in his body.

She strokes his face and his hair. "Your father isn't like you. Forget him, my child. This is my final word on the matter. Now, let's talk about something else." Refusing to let go, the duke presses on.

"But what if I can get him to repent for his sins? I mean, truly seek forgiveness?"

Taken aback by his suggestion, she ponders on it. Then she takes his hands into hers. "My son, I suppose if you can make this happen, then even the most wretched soul deserves a chance to redeem himself."

She does not want to disappoint him, but she is certain it will never happen and knows the verdict she will deliver at Henry's sentencing. It's what he deserves. God's justice for all the wrongs he has committed.

CHAPTER NINE
HALL OF MIRRORS

THE BRIDGETTINE MONK carries a lit torch in his right hand as he leads Henry through a labyrinth of dark subterranean catacombs. They stretch out for miles.

At first, Henry thinks they may have been used by the brothers to escape from his soldiers when Syon Abbey was taken over during the Reformation. Then, after a while, he pays little attention to the cold, bleak surroundings and follows the monk in silence.

When they make an abrupt stop, he bumps into the monk's back and is shaken out of his malaise. Thinking it must be a dead end of some kind, he peers over the man's shoulder to see what obstruction is ahead.

A large arched doorway takes up the entire space of the tunnel. The monk pulls a skeleton key from his habit pocket and hands it to Henry.

"Open it. They're all there. Waiting for you," he says, pointing at the door. These are the first words the monk has spoken in all the time they've been together, yet it seems clear that this is where their journey together ends. Henry is sure the monk will not accompany him beyond this point.

Henry struggles to unlock the door at first. Only after he presses his weight against it and gives it a hefty shove does the door finally creak open, and he stumbles into a large hall. Once inside, he feels disoriented by an infinite repetition of lit candles surrounding him. What is this place?

He reaches out to touch the candle closest to him, but rather than feel its heat, his hand hits a mirror. That's when he realises he is standing in a hall of mirrors. They cover every inch of every wall, the floor and the ceiling. This intrigues him.

It is not that he is unfamiliar with mirrors, but he has never seen anything like this before. A single candle burns in the centre of the hall, the source of the infinite and seemingly magical projection of candlelight. Puzzled by his reflection, he stares at the image of himself reflected back at him multiple times from every possible angle.

He appears tall, stocky, and much younger with wild, searching eyes. Despite his expensive clothing, he no longer looks like a king. The man who stares back at him looks bewildered and frazzled. A little on edge. Has he gone mad?

At that moment, the candle goes out. Henry is now in total darkness, surrounded by silence.

Alarmed, he looks for anything that might lead him back to the door through which he came, but he sees nothing but darkness. Or is there more?

Indistinct shapes and forms start to flicker and undulate inside the mirror closest to him. He can no longer see his reflection. Instead, distorted images emerge from behind it, gradually becoming one distinct image that comes alive.

He sees his father sitting behind his desk in the privy chamber at Richmond Palace. His father looks directly at him.

"Come here, my son," he seems to say.

"Sir?" Henry mutters in confusion, as if he needs permission to approach him. His father gestures to him to come to sit with him. Just like when he was little, like an obedient young boy, Henry walks toward him.

Strong emotions circle Henry like thick smoke. He almost falls, trembling from the fear and excitement of his father acknowledging him. He stops at the mirror and presses his hands and face against it.

He deeply respects his father and wants to get closer to him. This is very strange because they were never that close, but his desire to see him again is strong.

"There's too much we never spoke about," his father says.

Henry wants to say something in reply, but he feels as if he is thirteen years old again, awkward, shy, and in awe of this man whom he hardly knew.

"As of late, I feel you've withdrawn," his father continues. "You're more distant toward me, which I can understand considering everything that has happened to us as a family recently."

Henry concludes his father must be referring to the passing of Arthur and his mother.

"You're very much like your mother," his father observes. "You're wilful, just like her." His father looks him in the eye. He seems friendly and open but is still the king and the head of the family. "There were times when I thought you were too impatient and impetuous, but I realise now that you have your mother's temperament. She told me this once herself. She loved you for it, but it also worried her. Your mother was a very wise woman." His father's face shows great sadness.

"I miss her terribly," he continues. "In every possible way imaginable. She's my first thought in the morning and my last when I retire in the evening. We disagreed often, but on important matters, we stood united. To me, she was the most beautiful woman in all the world." He smiles at the thought of her face. "She was better educated than any man I knew and wiser too. Together we laid the foundations for a peaceful kingdom for many generations to come."

Henry's father looks at him with loving but sorrowful eyes. "My son, I didn't see you as often growing up as I should have. I know that now. I was closer to Arthur. He was more like me, both physically and emotionally, and I enjoyed seeing him preparing for his future role."

He falls quiet for a moment. "You always made me feel that I could trust you to be strong when matters required it." He pauses and looks down at his desk. "How could I have known that things would turn out the way they did?"

Henry is startled to hear his father speak like this. He almost wants to deny it, to tell his father that his emotional distance grieved him as a child but that, regardless of it, Henry respected him more than anyone in the entire world.

"I can, can't I? Trust you?" His father asks, then looks Henry in the eye as only a loving father can. "I want to believe you'll follow in my footsteps and make England the best it can be."

Henry nods, feeling as if he wants to cry and share with his father all the stories and heartaches that live inside him. The immense responsibility that rested on his shoulders for all these years and how lonely he felt. But it is not Henry's turn to speak.

"It's an incredible burden to be king," his father continues. "I tell myself that this is what I wanted and strived for. I gave everything I had for this. Twenty-four long and challenging hours each day for as long as I can remember. I've prayed for strength and guidance on so many occasions, and I'm still willing to sacrifice my own life if necessary." His father lets his hand slide over the desk as if brushing away the dust. His eyes are filled with pain.

"Sometimes I doubt if I can still keep it all together. Now that your mother's gone, I feel terribly alone."

Someone knocks on the king's door. His father looks up, disturbed. "Not now!" he cries out with a loud and angry voice. His father turns to Henry. There is an urgency about him. "I owe everything to God," he insists. "When I set foot on the Welsh shore at Mill Bay near Dale and Pembroke Castle, I came from France with only a small army. I was a fugitive who came with nothing: nothing but my faith. I arrived just before sunset on Sunday, August 7, in 1485. I kissed the ground and asked God to judge me and favour my cause. Two weeks later, I was the King of England, and that, my son, was God's will."

The tone in his father's voice, so full of conviction, gratitude, and love for God, makes a deep impression on Henry.

"I had one clear vision: to establish a Tudor dynasty ruling a united England. It was a vision your mother shared with me. Our marriage united the houses of York and Lancashire and laid the foundations for a long-lasting peace." For a moment, it looks as if he is remembering this vision.

"I always worked closely with Parliament to ensure I knew precisely what was going on in the country. I realised it's important to reward those who favour our cause and to infiltrate every level of society by paying the right people.

"I secured our wealth, and I knew every penny that came in and went out. I did everything to force loyalties and long-lasting alliances and to fend off those forces that oppose us and want to get rid of us. They're always there, Henry. Those who want to remove us and destroy everything." His father looks angry and upset.

"If they don't love you, or even hate you, make sure they can't afford to betray you," his father says, and he means it.

"Now for you, they tell me how lucky I am to have a son with such robust physical health. You possess natural athleticism and are capable in all sports. They also tell me you're intelligent and witty, loyal and generous, and enjoy discussions and debates. That's good. That's all very good indeed." His father smiles and seems pleased with this.

"I'm not a physical man, and I'll avoid direct combat if I can. Not only because I think we all have different talents granted to us by God, but I find it's my priority as a sovereign to survive and rule. Your brother, Arthur, was very much like me and understood this. My first and most important obligation is to carry on and protect myself, the king. Therefore, I'm not in favour of you participating in these jousting tournaments. It's mere entertainment, and it exposes you to unnecessary dangers. To be victorious as a king, you need to live life to the full." He speaks fervently, but Henry can tell his father is tired. Henry wants to ask him what is wrong with him. How can he help? But no words come out of his mouth.

His father stares at some papers on his desk, then rearranges them back and forth. When Henry tries to see what the papers are, he discovers there's nothing written on them. After a while, his father looks up from his desk. Then he stares off into the distance before he turns back to Henry. At that moment, Henry knows his father is about to tell him something important. He can see it in his eyes. They are filled with emotion: anguish and pain.

"I was alone in my chamber that night and sound asleep when a priest came to see me. The man seemed hesitant to speak. I became impatient and ordered him to be frank and tell me what the matter was. I wish I hadn't. I wish I never had to hear the words he was about to say."

His father stops for a moment, his head drooping forward. When he lifts it again, Henry sees that his father's eyes are filled with tears.

"He told me that if we receive good things at the hands of God, why may we not endure evil things? His words alarmed me, and I asked him what had happened. He said a boat had docked at Richmond Palace, and a messenger was on board with news from Ludlow Castle. I asked him again what kind of news. He told me that Arthur had departed to God." His voice cracks when he says it, and his lips quiver as he struggles to control his emotions.

"I heard him say these words, this awful truth. I must have screamed. I don't remember anything about it, but your mother rushed into the room in a panic. Later, after I shared the news with her, she reminded me that God had helped me to become king, and we'd have to find a way to carry on without Arthur."

Henry watches with despair as his father starts to weep.

"I've always felt I walked closely with God," his father says. "The Holy Spirit moved me many times and inspired me to act. But ever since that day, I haven't been able to pray in a true spiritual way. I feel I've lost my faith."

There is no time to reflect on this. A strong rush of air blows out all the candles in the room, Making Henry's father and the entire scene disappear, plunging Henry back into the dark.

CHAPTER TEN
FAMILY TIES

A DOOR INSIDE an adjacent mirror opens suddenly, and a beam of light creates the outline of a tall young man, not unlike Henry, who stands in the opening. Behind him is another man. As they move closer, Henry tries to get a good look at their faces. Where has he seen them before?

"You don't recognise me, do you?" the tall young man asks. Henry smiles. The voice gives him away. It is his brother, Arthur. Of course, it is. The long, smooth, intelligent face, the clear and gentle eyes, the fair hair and the boyish posture. Of course, this is Henry's brother. How could it not be?

"You look different," Henry says. "Older than I remember."

"Perhaps," Arthur replies. "I've left it all behind. Everything."

This sounds very cryptic. Henry does not know how to take it. He looks around the chamber where Arthur and his companion are. It is a library of sorts and has a striking resemblance to the one at Ludlow Castle.

"I'm still Arthur, but yet I'm not. You see, I have no desire to be a king anymore or to be married to Catherine, your wife."

Henry is taken aback by his brother's direct approach and unsure about the direction of this conversion.

"I don't understand what you're saying," Henry says hesitantly.

"No, you don't," Arthur replies with a force that takes Henry by surprise. "It was a momentous mistake. Brother, I should've been you, and you should've been me."

This does not make any sense.

"I never wanted to be king, and I didn't want to get married. That's why I say you should've been me, and I should've been you,"

Listening to Arthur confuses Henry. He feels he needs to explain things to him, the way he sees them.

"You died young," Henry says. "There was no one who wanted that or who is to blame for what took place."

Arthur shakes his head. "I didn't want to be king in the first place."

"But why?" Henry asks. "You didn't want to be Duke of Cornwall, Prince of Wales, Earl of Chester, Knight of the Bath and Knight of the Garter? Do you mean all of that meant nothing to you?" Arthur shakes his head. Henry cannot for one moment see any truth in this.

"This is all nonsense," he says.

Arthur smiles, not in amusement but in a sad way. Then, in a quiet voice, he tries to explain. "As a child, I enjoyed the attention. I loved our mother. I wanted to make her and our dear father proud, and for a long time, I thought that to become king was indeed what I wanted for myself, that it was my dream. But it wasn't. It didn't suit my temperament. My true ambitions. My heart's desire." He turns to look at his companion, who smiles back at him. Henry is baffled by all of this.

"I realise I hardly know you," Henry says. "I cried for you after you died. You were my only brother. To lose you was a great loss for our family and our country." Henry pauses for a moment as he recalls the moment his life changed forever. "It was I who was unprepared for what lay before me. At the time, I felt we were cursed and pleaded with God to return you to us so that you could take up your rightful place on the throne."

"I know," Arthur replies softly.

"Do you? You were our hope and inspiration." Henry is reassuring in his delivery. "I loved and looked up to you, even though I hardly saw or even spoke to you. I thought the world of you. You were going to be our very own King Arthur. I would have done anything for you."

There is a silent pause before Arthur responds.

"You all expected too much from me. I symbolised your hopes and dreams, but I could never live up to them. It just wasn't in me."

Henry finally recognises the tall, handsome man who is with Arthur. He steps forward and stands beside Arthur.

"The legendary Sir Gruffydd ap Rhys," Henry says with a degree of sarcasm. Why is he here? The nobleman nods but remains silent.

Henry remembers he was Arthur's closest friend and companion. The man's family was known to be unruly but decisive in his father's battle of Bosworth against Richard. The man's father, known as the uncrowned ruler of Wales, brought an army together larger than Henry's father's. They were trained and ruthless fighters.

"Our family greatly appreciated your father's support," Henry says.

"He killed the boar and shaved his head," Gruffydd says.

Of course, he means to say that it was Gruffydd's father who single-handedly killed King Richard in the marsh and that the fight had been bitter, the killing done gruesomely with a halberd, a combined spear and battle-axe.

"He lived his life as a true knight," Henry says.

"That's why our father thought we should be friends," Arthur says, smiling at Gruffydd. Gruffydd responds by resting his hand affectionately on Arthur's back.

The intimacy between the two men strikes Henry as odd, even though he has always been aware of their close bond. On the rare occasion he would meet Arthur, Gruffydd was always there with him. The two were inseparable. This was not unusual for young men, and Henry envied it. Their friendship struck him as honourable and noble.

Unlike Arthur, Henry did not have his own household far away from their parents. He was usually stuck inside the palace with his mother and his sisters.

He also remembers it was Gruffydd who came with Arthur to welcome Catherine when she arrived in London, and it was Gruffydd who accompanied the two back to Ludlow Castle in Wales afterwards.

Gruffydd was also the principal mourner after Arthur's tragic death months later. The nobleman travelled with the torch-lit procession from Ludlow to Worcester. Dressed in black, he rode a black-caparisoned courser, bearing Arthur's banner, which he also carried during the funeral service.

Upon Gruffydd's own untimely death, he was buried in Worcester Cathedral alongside Arthur's tomb, as it had been arranged between them.

Henry looks at Arthur. He still does not understand what Arthur is trying to say.

"I thought you were excited about meeting Catherine and enjoyed the wedding," Henry says. "I truly thought you did. The colourful pageants, the music, the dancing, the games, the people. You did, didn't you?"

Arthur exchanges a glance with Gruffydd.

"I thought I did. That's true. There was so much going on. Everybody was so excited about it all." Arthur turns away from Henry. "Gruffydd is older than me, and he understood me and everything so much better than I did then." Arthur turns toward Gruffydd. "Our bond has been more important to me than anything else in the world." The two men stare intently at each other as if to acknowledge a private understanding between them. Confused by the remark, Henry's fiery temper surfaces.

"What about Catherine?" he insists. "Did you consummate the marriage?" Arthur is about to speak, but then he changes his mind.

"Tell me," Henry demands. "You haven't made any sense in any way so far. Tell me. Did you or didn't you?"

"I was confused at the time," Arthur says, glancing at Gruffydd.

"Confused about Catherine?" Henry asks. Arthur shakes his head but stays quiet. This angers Henry even more.

"Why don't you tell me what happened?"

"It's not the truth you're after," Arthur says. "All you want is to condemn her. To be proved right."

This is ridiculous. Henry knows this is not true. "They say you boasted about it the next morning. It's on record. You told your servant: 'Bring me a cup of ale, for last night I was in the midst of Spain.' And you told everyone present: 'Masters, it's a good pastime to have a wife.'"

Arthur looks at him, resigned and embarrassed about the statement he had made at the time. Gruffydd steps forward. He is furious.

"If you value facts and truth so much, let me ask you this: why did you accuse my son of treason even though you knew it wasn't true? Why did you execute him?"

"Your son?" Henry asks. He tries to remember the situation. Rhys ap Griffith was Gruffydd's son. It was his only child from his marriage with Catherine St John. His son was not intelligent and certainly not helpful in any way, not to Henry, Gruffydd, or his family. The young man was reckless, a rebel and of no value to the country. What could Henry have done? Let this rascal create havoc in Wales?

"You died ten years before all of this took place. How can you possibly know what transpired after your death?" Henry asks.

"You falsely accused him. That's what you did. After everything my family did for you and your father. You're not worthy of being a king. You betrayed everyone who ever cared for you."

A fury erupts inside Henry. How dare this man throw such accusations at him? He is ready to confront the man, but before he gets a chance to vent his anger, everything turns pitch dark.

Henry is frantic, wondering how much more he can take. Then, from inside yet another mirror, he sees a sumptuous chamber materialise with a stately four-poster bed in the middle.

A youthful and graceful Elizabeth of York, his mother, born a princess, and Queen of England, lies in bed, holding a white rose in her still hands.

"Mother," he whispers, transfixed by the scene. He watches how she lies there in peace with so much strength and beauty, just as he remembers it.

A wave of buried emotions from that day so long ago resurfaces. He struggles to breathe as he relives her death, and it chokes the air from his lungs. He touches the mirror, moved by the raw honesty of his childhood experience.

It happened soon after Arthur's passing. As the only surviving son, it felt like life had stopped, and all hope was lost. Henry lost not only his mother but also the foundation of his family life and the stability it provided. Indeed, it marked the end of his childhood.

"No…" Henry does not hold back his tears. He cries out in pain, as he did back then. He was eleven years old when she died—just a boy. The wound never healed, even after all these years.

Suddenly, the entire ceiling cracks and breaks apart like a giant force destroyed it in anger. A massive volume of water, like a waterfall, rushes through it from above and into the hall.

Strangely, the water never reaches the ground. Instead, it hovers a metre above the floor and remains static, despite its sheer force and power.

Nestled inside the mass of water are etheric flames of light. Initially, they vibrate a soft mixture of white, sapphire and topaz, but not much later, they start to glitter radiantly.

Henry is within touching distance, yet when he stretches out to touch it, he cannot. This large body of water has created a world inside a world. A power greater than he has ever witnessed seems to live inside of it.

Within the body of water, his mother becomes visible again. Only now she is alive and dressed in a white robe, her long flowing hair hanging loose.

The invisible force lifts and carries her body in a slow and gentle motion. As she floats through the water in a slow, protracted movement, her arms are stretched wide open as if she is about to fly.

While Henry observes this phenomenal spectacle, she looks at him and smiles with joy. His heart is uplifted to see the woman who gave him life so happy again. It is a precious vision, meant for his eyes only, as the light of what could be a thousand stars envelops her.

Transfixed and in awe, Henry follows her journey upwards until she disappears through the open ceiling into heaven.

"I love you, Mama!" he shouts. "I'll always love you!"

After her departure, the lights within the water start to dim while the water becomes increasingly turbulent. Soon the large body of water starts to lose its shape, and its structure begins to collapse. It hits the floor with brutal force, and the cascade of water knocks Henry off his feet and floods the hall.

As the water level rises, Henry's senses are diverted by the distant sound of trumpets combined with a vision of his casket being lowered into the vault in Windsor Chapel. The eulogy is said, and the requiem Mass is concluded. The chief officers of the king's household break their staves of office and throw them into the vault to signal the end of their service.

He screams in anguish, and at that moment, he releases the pain, anger, bitterness and tears of all that is lost and gone. Soon the water comes up to his neck and then up to his mouth. It tastes salty, like the sea, and it is not long before he is dragged under water completely and taken deep underground.

REFLECTION

CHAPTER ELEVEN
ANNE'S UTOPIA

A NNE'S LAST MOMENTS on the scaffold were a blur of colours, sounds and emotions. The women with Anne removed her mantle and replaced her gable hood with a linen cap, under which she collected her hair to expose her neck. She thanked the ladies and asked them to pray for her.

The executioner asked her to kneel. She did but kept looking over her shoulder, worried that her coif would get in the way. With his deep voice, he told her not to be afraid and then waited until she was ready.

He approached her from behind and removed his shoes to minimise her distress. His assistant handed him the sword. With both hands, he circled it around his head to create momentum before bringing it down. Her head was instantly severed from her neck and fell into the straw on the scaffold.

After the dreadful deed, the cannons along Tower Wharf were fired to signal that the queen was dead. One of her ladies threw a white handkerchief over her head. Another picked up her head while weeping, and three more wrapped Anne's body in a white sackcloth.

Her body was then placed into a chest that was carried inside the Chapel of St Peter ad Vincula on the Tower grounds. That afternoon, after a priest delivered a final blessing, she was buried beneath the chancel pavement.

The passing itself was like being rocked to sleep. A peace enveloped Anne's soul to begin with. The angels were a vision in white and wrapped themselves lovingly around her, caressing her face as they whispered, "Don't be afraid," in soft tones. They attended to her and provided the care and protection her soul needed. It was a welcome relief after the terror and the heartbreak of being separated from Elizabeth.

All her emotions are reflected in the manor house she inhabits now, which, for the most part, is empty and deserted. When she feels sad and dreary, life is sucked out of her surroundings, colours fade, and straight lines and curves blend to become dark, cold enclaves. Creaking doors bang without rhyme or reason, and there are other strange noises that can't be explained. On occasion, a young child can be heard whimpering. Anne understands the house is somehow alive and that it responds to her pain and sorrow.

Most of all, she dreads the nightly ritual that will not stop. As she tosses in her bed, unable to sleep, a single candle flame casts grotesque gargoyle-like caricatures on the walls of her boudoir. She has trained herself to turn away from them.

As the night progresses, there is less and less order to her reality and a disappearance of structure. All of this is merely an appetiser for the anger and rage to follow. The wrong person's head was severed; that much is clear to her.

The savagery she experienced at the hands of the men who plotted her downfall was wrong. They should have been the ones to be judged, hanged, and quartered. Instead, they chose her, a queen and joyful soul with no wish other than to love and live. How can she ever reconcile what took place?

Revenge consumes her, and then, like clockwork, self-doubt hits her like a tidal wave as she contemplates how she could have done things differently. But that's not all. What comes next is the shame that she is to blame for everything.

She has been selfish, naïve, rebellious and provocative, too flirtatious perhaps, covetous and even spiteful. She should never have accepted the notion that she could usurp Queen Catherine. That was her fatal error, and it poisoned her mind. She lost clarity as a result. But what could she have done instead? Become his mistress, as her sister did?

Humans, even reasonable and responsible ones, can throw caution to the wind and risk everything they have in a single heartbeat. She witnessed how capable and intelligent men felt a sudden urge to speak truth to power even though they had none of the latter, often with disastrous consequences. So, when she felt cornered by the king's desires and lust, she changed her strategy on an impulse and decided to have it all by demanding from him the status of being his wife and queen. It was a bold and ambitious move on her part.

A dark feeling closes in on her. It was arrogant and foolish to think she could control him. Because of her, the entire Boleyn family, the anchor in her life, was annihilated. Its power and influence on the earthly plane were gone forever, and she and her brother were killed.

If only she could see her father and speak to him once more. To look into his loving eyes for just a moment and tell him how sorry she is. He would surely help her to remember her goodness. As his little girl, she had hoped for love and a good marriage that would make him proud of her.

She feels overcome with gloom and fears for her sanity. Her thoughts are with Elizabeth now. It is such a punishment not to be there to see her grow up, not to know she is safe or be able to comfort her through the dark days. Tears roll down her face, but they do not bring release. On the contrary, they make her suffering even more unbearable. Then, just as she anticipates, the candle flame blows out, and the room turns icy cold.

She shivers in the dark and cajoles herself to calm down and not give in to this evil torture. It helps. The cold disappears, and the candle flame reignites as if by magic.

Later, after she gets up in the middle of the night and stands in her boudoir in her long white nightdress, her purpose becomes clear. A feeling of resolve takes hold of her. She must fight to correct the wrongs of this travesty of justice put upon her by an immoral world. She calls her lady-in-waiting, an ageing, plain woman who came with the manor, to help her get dressed.

That morning, Anne sits at her bureau inside her drawing room. The few windows in the room are tall, but the shutters remain closed. Candles provide some degree of light, but it is sparse and subdued, just enough to observe the decor.

The threadbare carpets and aged green walls look sombre and neglected. The cracked golden paint on the wooden panelling, sculpted fixtures and elaborate stucco decorations hint at what once was a grand chamber. Additional pieces of tattered furniture and a chipped porcelain ointment jar that sits on top of the fireplace next to a silver gilt cup add to the atmosphere of crumbling wealth, but Anne doesn't seem to care about any of this decay.

A far more personal object is the rosewood writing box sitting on the bureau. Her white falcon emblem has been painted on its lid with the words "Most Happy" written beneath it. The box is a mysterious object with its many compartments, pens and a secret or two. Next to it are several other items, some blank parchment paper, an inkwell, a string of pearls and an ornately carved comb made of bone.

As she observes her pitiful surroundings, the thought of living like a recluse in a mausoleum amuses her. *This is all going to change,* she tells herself. She will have to imagine a new world to live in, design her own paradise, and when all the writing is done and the sketches complete, she will build her own Utopia. She giggles at the irony of her choice of name and contemplates what needs to be done.

Her ideal world will have to be a democracy, she decides as she takes a quill pen from the writing box and dips it into the inkwell. With large black letters, she scratches the word "Democracy" onto a piece of the parchment paper. A rush of excitement fills her spirit when she looks at the word on the paper. It is a declaration, a vision, yet there is a problem. In this world, her Utopia, her own position as the queen should be anchored in its constitution. This dilemma tempers her enthusiasm somewhat. She may have to write her own version of a *Magna Carta* with the rights of individuals and their freedom secured.

She picks up her quill pen again and writes down three more concepts on the paper: "Queen Anne, Parliament, *Magna Carta*." She draws a fat line under the word "Parliament." The details will come later. Maybe she can find a modern scholar to advise her on the matter.

The next group of ideals come easily, and she writes them down: "Love, God, Country, Family and Peace." She sits back and stares at the list for a long time. Something is missing.

Like a bolt of lightning, a thought pops into her head, and she smiles upon realising that this idea will complete the list. She writes and underscores "The Empowerment of Women." She sighs deeply and reflects on it for a moment. She feels this is one of the most consequential keystones of her Utopia. Her sex had been such a disadvantage to her while alive but not in this realm. Indeed, quite the opposite.

Anne's attention is drawn to the adjacent room. It's as if a voice speaks to her and begs her to come. She gets up from her bureau and enters the room through a connecting door.

This small space is her sanctuary, filled with freshly picked lilies of the valley, a favourite of hers. The air carries the flowers' sweet fragrance, conjuring fond memories of spring.

The room is lit with many candles of varying heights and feels sacred. An altar dominates the room. It is a decadent piece. Next to it hangs her most valued possession: a portrait of Elizabeth. The toddler in the picture smiles sweetly. As Anne stares into her child's eyes, flashes of the past fill her mind, and she remembers how she would hold Elizabeth. If only she could breathe life into the painting.

On the altar is a large silver cross encrusted with diamonds and gemstones, and a white mounted falcon on a stand. The prayer bench is upholstered in white velvet, and the long, heavy drapes made from white satin are embroidered with white roses. It is a rich display of feminine beauty, a hallmark of her taste for finer things.

Anne kneels on the bench and starts to pray. Soon her prayer turns into a private conversation with her daughter. Excited, she shares her ideas about Utopia and tells Elizabeth how much she loves and thinks of her. She hopes Elizabeth will grow up to be strong, independent, and loved by people. As tears stream down her cheeks, the candles blow out all at once.

CHAPTER TWELVE
REUNION

DESPITE HER SOLITUDE, Anne is not always alone. She
has her lady-in-waiting, of course, who attends to her needs.
Then there are the ghosts from her past.

Preferring her own company, she often refuses visitors who
come to see her, even her brother George, who has made many
attempts to call on her since her arrival. His presence is always
there in the background. She knows she only has to open the door
to him in her mind, and he will walk in and start a conversation
with her as if it were yesterday. But she does not want to see him.
Not yet. Indeed, she dreads it.

"The best thing that unites us is our father," she once told him
when they were still alive. He sympathetically agreed with her
but added that there was so much more between them. He then
started a long and articulate speech about the Reformation and
how he envisioned the country's future, once independent from
Rome, and their place in it.

She was excited to witness his growing interest in the
Reformation. She believed it would help give him a purpose
beyond the trifling ambitions of the court.

She accused him of being insatiable, which indeed he was,
whether in political debate, horse riding, gambling or in the pursuit
of carnal pleasures. She recognised so much of herself in George.
Both of them exuded a European sophistication, and they shared a
love of art and devotional literature. Yet they were vastly different.

Her enthusiasm and joyful spirit could be combative and, at times, provocative, just like him, but for her, the core of her being was not about winning but about love. His, in contrast, was to have the upper hand in everything. She admired and respected him for it and yet envied him.

He was a man, of course, a privileged one at that and could do what he wanted. But he was kind, and his humour was uplifting.

He privately joked about Cromwell calling him "*notre crapaud*," our pompous toad. He would add that "the man has no sense of humour and talks like a butcher with a speech impediment." It was hilarious, but even George had to accept that Cromwell was by far the most powerful man in the country, apart from the king, of course.

As lord warden of the *Cinque Ports*, George wrote Cromwell a furious letter and lectured the minister on how he should not try to subvert his position as a warden by his actions and warned him he was not taking this lightly. George felt superior to the man in many ways, and she agreed that her brother surpassed Cromwell in class, intellect and charisma.

She wonders if she should see George later that afternoon. Her lady-in-waiting confirmed his presence again. Yes, the afternoon will be good. That will give her more time.

She opens one of the drawing room shutters to assess the weather. The sky looks dark and ominous. A storm is on the way.

The park and the forest in the distance seem to have lost their colour, but she does not seem to notice, nor does she notice the roses in the garden, which look pale and dull, beginning to curl up.

Anne closes the shutter. She is restless and tired but decides she can work more on the new world she is imagining. Maybe she should not see George today. Her indecisiveness forms a part of her daily routine. Yes, no, maybe, and in the end, nothing takes place. She does not open the door to him, and they don't meet or talk. It is all left for another day.

There is always tomorrow, she tells herself as she pours a port wine from the clay jug into a floral Venetian goblet that sits on the side table, always half full.

A fire has been lit in her boudoir. Her lady-in-waiting holds up the hand mirror as Anne examines her yellow satin bodice and skirt. She looks joyful and carries her long dark hair loosely over her shoulders. Her iconic pearl necklace with the three drops and the golden initial "B" looks striking against the sumptuous silk fabric.

She puts several golden rings on but then changes her mind and removes them.

"I'd like to receive my brother, George, in the drawing room," she says, then returns the mirror to her lady-in-waiting.

"Now, your Majesty?" the woman asks, astonished. "It's seven o'clock in the morning."

Anne sits in the drawing room, waiting for George. "He's late," she says. He always was a poor timekeeper. Her heart races. What if he's angry with her? What if he believes it was her vanity that brought him down? What if he wants answers for all of it? Answers she cannot give him?

She squirms in her chair and realises it is a mistake to see him. She rings the bell for her lady-in-waiting to inform her of her change of heart, but it is too late. The door opens, and George enters the drawing room and bows in reverence to her status.

He has lost a considerable amount of weight, and there is some grey in his hair, but as always, he looks handsome in his white silk shirt, frilled at the neck and wrists under a tight-fitting doublet, with close-fitting breeches to match.

"George," she says, trying to hide her anxiety as she speaks his name.

"My dearest sister… finally."

"You look well," she says as she tries to control her trembling. George shakes his head.

"Thank you, but no. I've lost all of my exuberance. I'm no longer the man I once was." He looks almost defeated as he says it.

"You should be ashamed of yourself," he says after a brief moment of awkward silence, then tries to sound light-hearted and playful as if he is teasing her. "Are you in mourning?"

"My dress? What's wrong with it?" Anne is irked by his remark since she had made an effort not to look dreary.

He nods. There is a twinkle in his eyes. This is something they used to do: tease one another in a light-hearted way.

She starts to sob. "I've lost Elizabeth," she says, unable to control her emotions any longer. George's cheerful demeanour changes.

"I'm so sorry," she says. "It's been so hard. I hardly know how I get myself through each day."

Anne's sorrow affects George deeply. He looks at her and focuses on her pearl necklace with the golden "B." She feels self-conscious and notices him staring at it, so she touches her necklace as if to straighten it. There is a gentle acknowledgement between them.

"Elizabeth's a feisty little girl," he says. "She's a survivor and strong. She'll be fine."

"I tell myself that too. I know I have to believe that," Anne says, then walks toward one of the doors. "Come with me," she says, leading George into her private sanctuary.

CHAPTER THIRTEEN
GEORGE'S PAIN

GEORGE IS QUIET, and she can tell he is moved by the portrait of his niece hanging on the wall in the sanctuary. He slides his hand over the silk christening gown that Anne holds in her hands.

"I carried the canopy during the baptism in Greenwich," he says. "It gave me such a feeling of joy. Elizabeth is a dear, sweet little girl."

"She grew very fond of you, George," Anne replies with a smile. He nods with approval as he remembers Elizabeth's playful nature.

"The little rascal," he says, chuckling.

Watching him, she is reminded of everything that once mattered to her. The world and the family they once shared. The joy it gave her to have him in her life as the brother in whom she could confide. When she was faced with the dilemma of what to do about the king's marriage proposal and she asked him about it, he agreed with her ambitious plan to become queen.

She had second thoughts and would never have pursued it without his and their father's consent. It could never be merely about herself. Marrying the king would be her gift to the two men she loved most.

When they re-enter the drawing room, George's eye is drawn to the papers and sketches that are strewn across her bureau.

"May I?"

She nods. He walks over to the bureau and picks up a sheet of paper with lots of writing scrawled on it. Then, rather disparagingly, he shakes his head. "Your handwriting, my darling..."

"I know you don't like it," she says, smiling.

"It's not that. It lacks elegance. It's so whimsical, so unsteady, like a child's." He is amused by it. He could always find her weak spot, and she never liked it. George chuckles.

"That's not how everybody saw you," he adds. Anne looks surprised.

"Really?"

"They all thought you were fiery and very certain of yourself. Indeed, someone who felt she was way above her station. A schemer." This makes her laugh a little.

"That's how they saw you, George."

"Me?" Now they both laugh. It is the first time since her arrival that she has expressed any joy.

"Come to think of it, maybe we lofty Boleyns are all the same," he says. "Superior and full of ourselves."

She does not respond. Something has distracted her. George notices it but, at the same time, misreads it.

"They were betting ten to one I would be acquitted," he says, looking at her. She is shocked that he would bring this up now and feels it is insensitive, even rude.

"I had all the arguments there. It was impossible to see it in any other way."

"George," she says. Her face looks stern and fragile at the same time. "I can't do this now. I don't want to talk about what happened." George is so fired up he ignores her objections at first. After all, he, too, paid with his life for the false allegation of incest Cromwell had made against them.

"Even our father hoped I could be saved."

"George. Please. I must insist." She stands up to take charge of the situation. "I don't want to have this conversation right now."

George is baffled. In his eyes, she can see he notices her distress. He looks concerned and concedes, then quickly changes the subject. "I've thought about breeding horses again," he says. "There's only that many shuffleboard games one can play by oneself before it all seems like a terrible waste of time. My life feels very much in limbo here. Everything becomes frivolous after a while. I'm sure you understand what I mean."

He turns to look at the paper, the draft of the beginnings of Anne's constitution.

"What's all this about? What's this Utopia?" He looks at her, intrigued. "I never considered you much of a Thomas More enthusiast," he adds with sarcasm, referring to the once-renowned philosopher and former lord chancellor.

"It's not about his vision," she says.

"As you are aware, Utopia means 'No Place,'" he says, and their eyes lock.

"I felt it was rather fitting to call this place that. To create it here, I mean. Look at where we are."

George looks around at their dreary surroundings. "You have a point, my dear." He glances through Anne's list. He contemplates the first few keystones, then stops at "The Empowerment of Women" and gives her a furtive smile. George hands the paper back to her.

"I'm afraid I will have to leave soon. I've overstayed my welcome."

She reaches out to him and adjusts his silk shirt. He likes it when she mothers him, and he allows it without making a fuss.

"Don't worry. You look immaculate as always," she says, smiling. George tenses up, and she notices a sudden feeling of unease in her brother's eyes as he avoids her stare.

"Do you have to go so soon? Why don't you stay a little while longer?" she asks. "There's still so much I need to speak of."

Despite all his brilliance and charm, she always knew something troubled her brother. It was as if he was born with a hunger he did not know how to satisfy.

At first, she thought it was his youth, inexperience or maybe even talent. She had noticed this with other great minds, that often there is a shadow, a darkness they can't control, like a storm that cannot be tempered.

Her brother, with his dark eyes, sits opposite her. The fire she normally finds in those eyes is gone. Instead, she senses a sadness that comes from a deep place inside. Something they have in common. She smiles, encouraging him to speak.

After a long pause, he asks her a question out of the blue.

"Was it because of me?"

Numb, she stares at him in disbelief. Why does he ask her this?

"Did I cause offence?"

The muscles in her neck and jaw stiffen, and a coldness enters her heart.

"I thought you and I could do great things together and change our country. I can now see that I've been reckless and ignored my responsibility as your elder brother to take care of you. I've been selfish."

"Stop," she whispers.

"No, it's important for me to speak. Please, allow me," he says, looking at her with anguish.

She looks down and dreads what more he will say.

"I grossly overestimated my importance. I made the error of trusting in the vanity of the world, especially in the flattery of the court. Through my shortcomings, I was unable to see through them. As a result, I gave you the wrong guidance. I should've warned you of the betrayal of others and the dark forces around us. Instead, I fed you with the same desire for power that lived in me."

When she looks at him again, she notices the tears in his eyes. Instantly, she remembers her deep love for him.

"It's not true." Her voice is calm and gentle. Reassuring. "It wasn't because of you. It never was."

In response, George lets out a wail of anguish and bursts into tears. Ashamed, he hides his face in his hands. "I would've given everything to save you," he sobs.

"I know that," she says. Anne leans lovingly over to her brother and takes his hands in hers. "You'll always be my cherished brother. I love you."

George looks at her with deep affection and strokes her hand.

"You're a beautiful soul, Anne," he says. "Why are you still here in Limbo?"

His question catches her off guard. Filled with emotion, she shakes her head.

"Tell me," he continues. "Why are you by yourself? We all love you and miss you."

"I'm not ready yet," she says. Without understanding why, she knows her time has not yet come to leave.

Dawn has arrived and creeps in through the cracks of the shutters. They both notice it. George gets up and extends his arms to her. "Come here." They embrace each other.

"Are you sure you don't need help with Utopia?" he asks. "I could write a beautiful charter of rights for it."

She laughs. "I know you could, but this is my project. My world. Now go!"

CHAPTER FOURTEEN
REMEMBRANCE

DURING HER TRIUMPH at becoming queen, the River
Thames played an important role in the celebrations. On
the day before the coronation, a procession of about fifty barges
decorated with red and white roses, flags, streamers and banners
rowed in unison down the Thames to Greenwich. Anne, who was
on her way to meet Henry, was overjoyed to be at the centre of
such a marvellous spectacle.

At one point, the royal barge was surrounded by a fleet of
passenger boats and rowboats packed with excited passengers
while colourful dragons and fireworks filled the May sky.

From Greenwich, she travelled over water to the Tower of
London where all the lords of England received her, no longer as
Lady Anne, Marquess of Pembroke, a title Henry had given her
in September the year before, but as Queen of England. Her new
status thrilled her, but it was not only that. It was the way they all
stared at her, mesmerised by her presence.

When she landed, a thousand gunshots were fired from the
Tower and many more from the ships floating on the Thames.
Henry came out to meet her and embraced her firmly. He was
over the moon, like a teenage boy. He kissed her in the most
spontaneous and romantic way.

She felt empowered, even emboldened, by his desire for her.
She had never felt happier than on that day. Her pregnancy had
hastened the couple's secret marriage and her coronation. Henry,
of course, did not want anyone to doubt the legitimacy of the son

he hoped for.

Two days later, she rode from the Tower through the city to Westminster Palace in a rich chariot with silver cloth covering her head. She was accompanied by a large following that included lords, knights and gentlemen, four chariots of ladies and several other ladies riding on horseback, all in gowns made of crimson velvet.

Here and there, she heard insults shouted at her and mocking laughter from some bystanders lining the streets. She ignored it. Those loyal to Catherine and the Roman Catholic Church were large in number, but their cause was lost. This was Anne's triumph and that of the Reformation, and nothing would deter her.

The next day, on June 1, she walked down the aisle in Westminster Abbey toward the altar under a canopy of gold cloth, dressed in a kirtle of crimson velvet decorated with ermine and a purple robe draped over her shoulders. She wore a rich coronet with a cap of pearls and stones upon her head. The rather elderly Duchess of Norfolk carried her train in a robe of scarlet with a gold coronet on her cap, and Lord Burgh, her chamberlain, supported the train in the middle.

Behind her followed ten ladies in robes of scarlet trimmed with ermine and gold coronets on their heads. After them, walked all her maids in gowns of scarlet edged with white Baltic fur.

Seated on a high platform before the altar, Anne was anointed and crowned Queen of England by the Archbishop of Canterbury and the Archbishop of York. It was a glorious moment. *Their* moment.

Utopia, she decides, needs a river as well, just like the Thames, for the festive celebrations that she plans to host. A miniature model of Utopia needs to be built. She finds an empty chamber in her residence that is perfect for it. The chamber is spacious with windows overlooking the rear landscaped garden. In the middle, a large dining table serves as a high podium.

Anne imagines the city will have classical architecture inspired by Nineveh, the old city from the Book of Jonah built along the Tigris River.

There will be many boats on the water and palm trees on the riverbanks, with horses, sheep and goats grazing on the land. Multi-layered ancient temples and palaces will rise from the river. At many vantage points, large marble steps will grant visitors access to the city from the boats moored in the harbour.

Within the city, she imagines a network of canals and aqueducts providing vital water and sanitation for Utopia's citizens, and water to irrigate the Italian hanging gardens, tiered parks, waterfalls and terraces that will sustain a wide variety of foliage, exotic fruits and flowers.

When she leaves the chamber, only to return moments later, the model of Utopia has come alive. It is as if a skilled architect and his team of assistants have worked their magic. It is complete. Anne stands before it and feels elated and proud. As she surveys her creation displayed on the large table in the room, sunlight pours in through the windows to create a warm and inviting stage. It takes her breath away. She smiles. This is a good omen.

She steps outside into the garden through an access door attached to the chamber to cut fresh flowers for Elizabeth's altar. She picks up a basket and some clippers from the ground. The sky is clear with a light breeze.

Hundreds of white roses are on display. At the far end of the garden are red roses as well. Inspired by the garden's beauty, she picks a mixture of red and white roses in honour of Elizabeth's heritage as a Tudor princess.

While cutting the roses, she remembers giving birth to Elizabeth at Greenwich Palace. The labour was arduous. She and Henry were convinced she would give birth to a son. Various physicians and astrologers had assured them of it. Henry took it badly, of course, and felt cheated once more, but for Anne, the initial confusion and disappointment were soon replaced with delight. Elizabeth was a healthy baby, and a prince would surely follow. She convinced him of it. "*Te Deums*" were sung at St Paul's the following day to mark the birth, and great preparations were made for the christening.

Without cause, her mood changes. A tiredness overwhelms her, and she starts to feel weary and has difficulty breathing. She stops cutting roses and looks up at the sky. An irregular and ominous dark cloud has formed in the sky, which was blue only moments earlier. *What kind of cloud is this?* she wonders.

It is not a cloud but an enormous plume of smoke. Anne searches the horizon for its origin. It is the forest in the distance. Is there a fire? Uncharacteristic of her inquisitive nature, she ignores it and takes the flowers inside.

The roses she cut need to be arranged. She separates the red and white stems into different vases that are then spread throughout Elizabeth's room. The red roses are positioned in an outer circle, with the white roses forming an inner circle. As she does this, she wonders whether her daughter will be able to remember her.

Distracted by her thoughts, Anne pricks her finger on a thorn, and it draws blood. She squirms at first but then stares at it as if something has happened that should not be possible before sucking her finger to ease the pain. After she arranges the flowers, the entire room is filled with them and their sweet bouquet. Anne is pleased.

It is already dark when her lady-in-waiting brings her a glass of water and suggests that Anne try to eat something. Anne refuses. All she desires is to sit in the dim room with a few candles, the large portrait of her little one, and surrounded by roses.

For hours she sits there, talking to herself and drifting in and out of her memories. They are all she has of her baby. She is filled with dismay at how things turned out. How blind she has been.

She does not include *him* much in her thoughts. She reluctantly agreed to be part of his trial shortly after his death and was curious to talk to him, but now she regrets it. Their meeting in the crypt left her bruised and empty. There was no healing and no peace from the encounter, and she decides that when the court reconvenes again for his sentence, she will not participate. She doesn't want to waste more time on the man who destroyed her. Instead, she thinks about the one who got away.

CHAPTER FIFTEEN
LOST AND FOUND

IN THOSE EARLY YEARS, Henry Percy, sixth Earl of Northumberland, was someone who stood out in a crowd. He was intelligent, wilful, sometimes dramatic and grandiose, and yet a truly gentle soul. At twenty years of age, he was five years older than her, and he fell deeply in love with her from the first time they met.

Percy was not as well-spoken or confident as her brother, but when she was introduced to him at court, she felt drawn to his strong physical presence and dry sense of humour.

He had already been knighted by the king and held a place in the household of Thomas Wolsey, the king's almoner, while Anne served in Queen Catherine's household.

She was flirtatious and captured Percy's heart with the long and frequent conversations they shared, which she took great pleasure in. He was kind and attentive, and they both felt that they were meant for each other. Kindred spirits.

They kept the relationship a secret. They had no choice. Percy was already betrothed to Lady Mary Talbot, daughter of the fourth Earl of Shrewsbury, and Anne was due to marry James Butler. Anne quickly learned to trust him and experienced a happiness and intimacy that were new to her.

Together they created their own little world, as romantics do, and it was not long before the tentative gestures and secret notes that passed between them turned into blunt, bold confessions and expressions of love. It was only natural they discussed the idea of marriage.

Percy was elated by the prospect, but when Wolsey discovered he had made a secret betrothal to Anne, he was forbidden to see her again and sent back home to marry Mary.

It was a brutal end to an idyllic time, and it devastated them both. They told her Percy fought against the decision and even cried openly with sorrow when it was clear that no one supported the idea of marriage. She was sent home to Hever Castle. Angry and heartbroken, she swore to seek revenge on Wolsey.

Callous men like Wolsey do not understand love or even care about the happiness of others. Life for them is merely a game of chess. Every move on the chessboard is strategic. Everything is reduced to dominance and power. Marriage, the most sacred union between a man and a woman, is no exception.

To her surprise, she can feel Percy's presence now. It is as if he wants to visit her. This could mean only one thing. He has crossed over. She refuses to believe it at first. Percy was ill in recent years, but she prefers to believe he is still alive. But even if he is not, what use could it be to see him?

She wonders if he was the love of her life as she was for him. Percy never made a secret of how he felt for her. But what about her?

Thinking about him makes her sad. After their painful separation and breakup, she lost what she felt for him at first. That initial spark and her admiration and complete devotion to Percy. How naïve she was then.

Being courted by the king and the attention and power that came with it were of a different calibre. The attention she received was all-consuming. Intoxicating. What woman could resist a king's flattery? She began to think that a man like Percy could never compete. In any case, he was now married to someone else, and their life together looked mundane and uneventful.

"Is that so?" A man's voice from behind her startles her. She recognises the voice immediately and turns around. Percy, with his broad shoulders, brown beard and fiery eyes, stands before her, just as he did all those years ago when she first met him. They look intently into each other's eyes.

"I disagree that true love can fade over time," he says.

"Percy," she says softly, extending her hands out to him. She is perplexed to see him and feels a mixture of joy and sadness. Shy, he takes her hands and kisses them.

"My dearest Anne," he says. "I know you still have feelings for me." Anne's heartbeat quickens, and she begins to perspire. She now knows this to be true but stubbornly pushes the thought away.

"I hoped you would outlive me with many more years," she says.

"Why?" Percy asks, somewhat surprised. "I never desired to live a long life. Not after I lost you and was forced to marry a woman I didn't love." Anne does not know how to respond to his confession.

"I thought of you just before you came. I remembered how you left me," she says, then hesitates, "It was like being forced to leave my home. I had nowhere to go—no one to confide in. Over time the wounds healed, and my feelings changed. Now, after years of being apart, I'm no longer the same person. Things are different now. What was lost can never be found." Tears well up in her eyes as she speaks.

"That's not true," Percy says. He is impatient with her now; she can tell.

"For me, it is," she says with regret. "I've lost everything. My heart. My soul. I'm in Limbo."

Through her tears, she looks at him. He regards her with agony. He calls her name and tells her again their love can never die and that the Anne he fell in love with and whom he will forever love is still there.

"I see her in your eyes. I feel her presence in my heart and long for her." She hears him say the words, but while she looks at him, she realises he knows it is untrue. He steps toward her and takes her hand.

"Let me help you get her back," he says, his face close to hers.

"Percy, you're the most generous, the most loyal and gentlest man I've ever known," she replies, then turns away. "I wish you'd accept this truth and not make me suffer any than I do already." Anne looks at the open door that Percy came through and the long corridor beyond it. She feels empty and alone. When she turns back and looks at him, Percy has changed. The unbearable truth has hit home. He releases her hand and looks at the floor. He's defeated.

"The last time I saw you was in court when you defended your honour," he says after a moment. "I couldn't believe how strong and courageous you were despite the betrayal of all those around you." His eyes reveal the admiration he felt for her that day. "Your light was such a contrast to the malice that had taken hold of the proceedings. I collapsed during the absurd spectacle. They had to carry me outside, so I missed part of it, something I still regret. I wanted to be there to support you."

"My love…" There is kindness in Anne's eyes and voice. "Tell me what happened to you. I would like to know what I can do to help."

"Why would you want to do anything for me?" Percy does not understand how she can say this now. She strokes his shoulder to reassure him.

"As you know, I got married, just as my father wanted. My wife and I fought each other bitterly from the start. She hated me as much as I hated being married to her. She petitioned to get an annulment, but it didn't succeed. Nevertheless, we lived separate lives. From then onwards, my health deteriorated. Breathing became especially difficult for me, and I was terribly lonely during those years without you. I often dreamt of the life we could have had together. The children we could have had. Anne…" Percy reaches out to her, but Anne takes a step back.

"I'm sorry," she says. "You'll have to let go of me."

He shakes his head. "I will not."

"You must if you are to escape this prison and find freedom for your soul. Do it for me," she pleads. "Please. It will help me to see you happy again." Percy stands in silence opposite her. There is despair in his eyes. "He was despised and rejected by mankind," Anne recites, "a man of suffering, and familiar with pain. Like one from whom people hide their faces, he was despised, and we held him in low esteem."

"Isaiah," he says.

"Will you pray with me?" she asks.

Percy nods. "Can I hold you at least one more time?"

She extends her arms to him, and together they find each other again.

"I love you," he whispers.

"I love you too," she whispers back.

Both of them will remember this moment forever.

CHAPTER SIXTEEN
OMENS

LIKE A RECLUSE who inhabits her private hideaway, Anne finds peace in her daily meditation. Earlier, she instructed her lady-in-waiting that no more visitors were welcome and that she must not be disturbed unless there was news of Elizabeth.

In the drawing room, she sits at her bureau and reads a passage from her book of hours with its colourful illustrations, but she cannot keep her focus for long.

All the papers relating to Utopia have either been pushed to one side or hidden inside the drawers. Just one piece of paper remains. On it, written in her handwriting, are the words: "My Dearest Elizabeth." Nothing more. Anne's pen rests next to the paper, waiting for more words to be written, but she lacks the inspiration, so nothing comes.

Frustrated, she gets up and walks over to the comfortable chair. As she leans back and stares at the ceiling, she points to the stucco decorations barely visible in the darkened room and tries to draw their outline with her finger. Her attention is fixated on the shapes made by the flickering candlelight, which dances across the ceiling.

It doesn't take long before the same old voices in her head begin to murmur in the background. They appear as random thoughts spoken with polite and hushed voices at first, but soon they turn into a mob of hostile, unruly characters who scream at her from the darkness. What on earth was she thinking? Queen of England?

She stretches her arms toward the ceiling. "Help me," she whispers. "Please help me." It's as if someone hears her plea, for tiny orbs of white light appear around her hands and circle her fingers. Together they form a fanciful pattern and move in every direction with a gentle flow.

"Heal me," she begs, moving her hands and fingers like a dancer trying to tell a story. A tale of reaching out to the source of all creation. The one true God.

A chill in the air disrupts this spiritual encounter. Her skin turns icy cold. Startled, she jerks her arms back. The temperature in the room drops even further. What or who has entered her space?

With a loud bang, one of the window shutters is thrown wide open, and strong wind blasts into the room. The candle is blown out, and several of the papers on her bureau flutter through the air. Leaves and dirt fly in from outside.

Paralysed with fear, she witnesses the chaos around her. The shutter slams against the wall, but still, she is too afraid to get up and close it.

Enough! She reprimands herself, and then finds the courage to get up and shut the window, but when she looks through the window into the night sky, she is frozen to the spot.

Violent images of lightning move from east to west. She recognises the images that take shape in the distance and gasps in horror.

"Death, war, famine and pestilence," she mutters. Her eyes follow the disturbing spectacle as the four horsemen of the apocalypse gallop across the sky. She realises they foreshadow the end of the world. Her world.

She shivers and wraps herself in a blanket. While sitting at the edge of the bed, horrified and confused, she tries to figure out what to do or what it all means, but a fog has entered her head, and her judgment is clouded. It exhausts her, and it gets so bad she has to lie down and close her eyes. The moment she lies back on the soft pillows, she falls into a deep sleep.

Anne awakens hours later with no recollection of who or where she is or any of the events before her sleep. She does not even remember her name for a moment, which causes her to question her sanity.

"You're Anne. Yes, that's right. Anne," she says. "You died, and now you're in Limbo."

A bright yellow locust as large as her hand sits on her bed and seems undeterred when she moves into an upright position. What is it doing in her room? A moment later, she spots another one on her desk.

This is strange. She picks up a book from her side table to swat the locust, but before she can get close, it flies up and starts circling the room, flapping its wings. The other locust takes off as well. One of them comes straight toward her. Still half asleep, she waves her hands in the air to shoo it away, but the locusts are persistent.

This annoys her terribly. She unlatches the shutters and wants to open the windows to get the locusts out. Her mouth drops open. Her beautiful garden. The forest. The entire outside world has been transformed. All the green of the grass, the plants, the shrubs and the trees have been stripped bare, and her beautiful roses are nothing but rows of naked stems and plucked heads.

The shock is so enormous that tears stream down her face. The world in front of her looks so bleak and deserted. It takes all her life and hope away.

In a blind panic, she calls for her lady-in-waiting and runs frantically through the house to open all the shutters and doors. Where did she leave the keys? When she opens the door to her drawing room, she is met by a swarm of locusts that have stripped all the soft furnishings bare.

The window is wide open. Horrified, her arms flailing, she attempts to drive the locusts out through the window. She checks the door to her private sanctuary. It is locked.

When she finally finds the keys, she discovers she is alone in the house. She opens all the shutters and doors, only to discover the large hall has also gone through a metamorphosis. The windows have cracked, and some of the glass lies scattered on the dusty wooden floor.

She looks through a broken window to see the remains of a dystopian world. It looks hostile and grim. Remarkably, the only thing left intact in all its splendour is the model of Utopia.

When she enters the chamber, she is taken aback by its sheer beauty. The temples, the river, the gardens, the canals, the palaces… it is all there, its beauty untouched by the devastation. But there is no time to admire it. Instead, she runs outside.

The first glimpse of dawn is visible in the sky, and a thick, damp mist rises from the ground. In the distance, Anne sees the swarm of locusts that ravaged her gardens fly away to the north. While investigating the damage, she makes the most disturbing discovery. The river that once flowed through the land and brought life to the surrounding flora and fauna is bone dry.

By the time she gets back inside the house, the locusts have left, but large cracks are visible on the walls. The world around her seems to be disintegrating. Worried, she inspects Elizabeth's room, which she did not get the chance to do before. Thankfully, everything is intact.

For the next few hours, she works tirelessly to remove the dirt, the dust and the remains of the infestation from the house.

CHAPTER SEVENTEEN
HOLY FIRE

HENRY IS sucked through the hall floor into a dark underground shaft. The experience that follows defies the laws of physics as he tumbles through dimensions of time and space in a circular motion for what seems like an eternity.

Objects appear and circle him. Most are familiar to him. Memories of documents and objects he once held or owned: elaborate maps of the seas that depict the world in great detail, numerous sketches of warships and their cannons, and extensive lists of trade and cargo; snapshots and smells of delicious foods from distant lands, shining gold and silver, exquisite fabrics and trinkets of every description, and luxurious tapestries.

The tapestries depict biblical characters like Saint Paul or Abraham and are meticulously woven with gold and silver thread. Some are more than twenty feet long. Like magic carpets, they wrap themselves around his body, and he shrieks in wonder as he imagines himself in the scenes they depict.

Sheets of music float past him, demanding his attention. As a musician who can sight-read music, he hears their tunes and revels in the melodies made by various instruments. This is followed by a chorus of angels who sing the chords. Their sound is sublime, and the words of the familiar songs they sing bring sweet memories that fill him with joy.

At some point, Henry finds himself in a large building made from white marble and crystal. It is full of beautiful women dressed in long white robes. They have gathered to sing songs of praise to

God. The light they radiate is pure love.

He is surprised to see Catherine among them. She looks confident and strong. Next to her sits his beloved wife, Jane Seymour. How radiant she looks. His immediate impulse is to call out to her, but when she turns her head toward him, she looks horrified. What or who does she see? Is it him?

From then onwards, everything becomes very confusing. He is tossed around like a young lad in a brutal football match. It is as if the vicious mob fighting for the opposing team are hellbent on ripping him apart.

The experience seems to continue for an eternity until he is spat out like Jonah from the belly of the whale.

Henry lands with a hard bump on a grass-covered hilltop. Wet, battered and bruised, he wonders what in God's name just happened.

Wherever it is, it looks like a good place to catch his breath and rest. From his high vantage point, he relishes the glorious sunrise in front of him and the mysterious valley below.

Above him, strips of pale blue and yellow sky intermingle with clouds saturated in shades of orange, pink and deep purple.

Where is this place? It must be England somewhere, and yet it doesn't seem real. Could it be heaven?

He believes he is still the king, the handsome and charismatic Tudor monarch who was powerful, grand and cultured in a way England had never seen before. But that was before he crossed over. Does any of it matter now? He convinces himself it does.

Apart from Charles V, Francis I or Suleiman the Magnificent, not many men alive could equal his accomplishments. Few could compete with his versatile talents and ability to transform and unite a country the way he did. A powerful independent nation-state, free from Rome and foreign interests. Who else could claim such a victory? No doubt history will judge his reign to be one of the greatest. A smile appears on his face.

His muscles relax after he takes a deep breath. He did well, he tells himself, and he finally feels he can let go for a moment. He lies down in the cool grass and dozes off.

Soon he falls into a deep trance, and the pain and aches in his body begin to subside and heal. This is all good.

The days end quickly here. The sun disappears below the horizon, and everything around him turns dark. Bright stars fill the sky, which is lit by a full, silvery moon.

All of this is followed in rapid succession with the break of a new day. In the east, the sun rises and then travels to its highest point before it completes its journey and sets in the west. This time a blood-orange moon appears in the sky, a rare omen, and night returns. The cycle repeats over and over again, and he remains still throughout, his eyes shut.

On occasion, it starts to rain but only briefly, and sometimes there are flashes of lightning, thunder and a strong wind that comes and goes. But he is detached from it all.

Ghostlike figures climb up from the valley below him. Some walk past him; others stay put and keep him company. Their etheric bodies are translucent, and their presence is in no way intrusive. He doesn't even know they are there.

Some come alone, others in groups, and all converse with one another in muffled voices. Their languages sound like music filled with foreign tones and melodic rhythms. They are dressed in costumes that have never been seen before, turning the hilltop into a marketplace of colour and mystery.

When Henry finally wakes up, it is dusk. He is no longer on the grass that overlooks the beautiful vista. Instead, there is a forest up ahead, and in the near distance, the remains of a wall covered in dead ivy. The iron gate attached to it has rusted over, and half of it is sunk into the ground.

Behind it lies a large square with limestone slabs splattered with mud. Weeds have sprouted everywhere, and small derelict, burnt-down buildings surround the square. Without thinking, he makes his way toward the square.

Smoke rises from some of the buildings around it. A howling wind blows overhead and creates moving silhouettes with the smoke that take the shape of ugly gargoyles and demons.

On the opposite side of the square, a lonely figure stands in the doorway of one of the smaller buildings. The figure disappears inside it, but Henry immediately recognises the black habit the figure is wearing. "Wait!" Henry cries out, hurrying after him. "I need to talk to you!"

He crosses the square and finds the monk sheltering in a small room inside the building, his back to Henry and the hood of his habit pulled down. When the monk turns around and steps into the light, Henry is shocked to see his face.

It is disfigured, and a deep scar runs across it. The man's nose and jaw have melted like wax, while one of his eyes is glazed over. An area of his neck is visible through the habit, revealing a large burn, partially healed with purple-black lesions.

"Your Majesty," the monk says. The voice gives him away. It is the same Bridgettine monk from Syon.

Taken aback by the monk's appearance, Henry is astonished but nevertheless pleased to see him.

"Where am I?" Henry asks.

The monk smiles mysteriously, and Henry wonders if he disrespects him or even pities him.

"The cortège left the abbey some time ago," the monk says. "Early in the morning, they took the casket with Your Majesty's body from the crypt and brought it to Windsor."

Henry knows this already, but the news still makes him depressed.

"For the funeral service, the chapel in Windsor was draped in black," the monk continues. "The coffin was lowered into the vault in the quire. Stephen Gardiner, Bishop of Winchester, said the eulogy and celebrated the requiem Mass while the dowager queen observed the ceremony from an oriel window. After the Mass, the trumpets sounded."

"Please spare me the rest," Henry says.

The monk nods.

"Where am I now? Where are the angels? Where is God?"

The monk looks at the ceiling in alarm. "Come," he says, his voice filled with urgency. "You need to get out of here."

In a split second, the whole situation around them changes. A large beam falls from above. It is on fire, and flames and smoke rapidly fill the small space.

"Quick. This way," the monk says as he stands at the doorway. Beyond it, shrieking voices come from the square.

Henry feels paralysed as he stares at the room's interior. Only moments ago, it was empty, but now there is a small wooden table in the centre. A large Bible lies open on top of it. A bed and a chair are positioned in the corner, and a crucifix hangs on the white wall. He is inside a monastic cell. Around him, the fire spreads, eventually consuming everything in the room.

"Come!" the monk shouts, pulling Henry out of the cell and into the square.

The entire monastery is on fire. The brothers' cells face the square, and a large communion hall between their private quarters is situated at the top end. An angry mob has taken over the square. Some of them are soldiers.

This is the dissolution of the monasteries ordered by Henry himself. This is the Reformation, the bloody liberation of the Church from the oppression of a foreign power, the pope.

The mob hurls stones, windows are broken, and entries are forced. Furniture is taken out, and books are thrown onto a pile and set on fire. Amidst it all, a man of the faith dressed in a white habit, who was praying in his cell moments before, is dragged through the mud. The mob scolds him and beats him. It is all very chaotic.

The drama reaches a crescendo when one of Henry's soldiers decapitates the beleaguered monk with a sword and then holds up the severed head, met by cheers from the mob.

"Stop!" Henry cries, but the crowd pushes him aside. When he tries again, someone hits him over the head.

He is sure he has collapsed to the ground, but moments later, he finds himself amidst a horde of people in London in the middle of the day.

This is not a dream; this is real. He is reliving what took place on his orders, an actual moment in time, but he is not experiencing it as the king. Henry is now just part of the crowd, a mere spectator with no rank or title. A commoner.

CHAPTER EIGHTEEN
HANGED, DRAWN AND
QUARTERED

H ENRY IS NOT FAR from the Tower, the imposing outer
wall behind him, and the White Tower standing high in the
distance. It is the fourth of May, 1535. How and why he knows
this is unclear, but he does. He understands what is going on and
also why he is part of it.

It all began with his divorce from Catherine and his marriage
to Anne. After that, it became much bigger.

During the dissolution of the monasteries, he revisited the
idea that in the long tradition of biblical kings, the monarch is
God's anointed representative on Earth. The king has a special
relationship with God. Just like King David before him, Henry
was part of this tradition. Consequently, he declared himself
supreme head of the Church of England in 1531. This was how
God intended it. Henry was and still is sure of this truth.

The Carthusian monks were outraged and openly resisted this
declaration. Many others agreed with them, but the Carthusian
monks were widely respected amongst the people, and their refusal
to acknowledge Henry's newly appointed status endangered not
only his authority but also the stability of the entire country.

As Henry's chief minister, Cromwell tried to reason with them. He
even offered the monks a substantial amount of money. When that
did not work either, Cromwell threatened and bullied them without
success. In the end, there was no alternative but to try them for treason.

The fourth of May was the start of a series of executions ordered by Cromwell to force any opposition to abide by the country's new law.

Three Carthusian monks in their white robes and a Bridgettine monk are the first to be executed. Guards from the Tower take them outside. It is the first time they meet each other after their imprisonment.

Henry stands amidst the curious crowd that has gathered outside the Tower. The monks look unafraid and calm. To Henry's surprise, they even smile at each other.

All the spectators around him have fallen quiet and observe the scene with interest. The monks display not even a hint of fear, appearing to have surrendered to their fate. Maybe they believe they are following in the footsteps of many of the great saints persecuted for their faith down the ages. That would be foolish, but these monks have already shown that they are stubborn.

"These blessed fathers are cheerfully going to their deaths," someone not far from Henry in the crowd says with a mixture of admiration and disbelief. It annoys Henry, but he has to admit that the monks' courage is impressive.

The guards take the prisoners to the horses with the hurdles that await them near the gate. The horses are restless, snorting and jostling each other. Growing impatient with the monks, the guards push them forward, then force them to lie down with their feet close to the horse on the higher end of the hurdle and tie them down.

Poor souls. Everyone present knows that the three-mile journey from the Tower to Tyburn, the place of execution, is going to be a tortuous and painful ordeal. The monks will be dragged through the streets over uneven cobblestones and through potholes filled with mud and human waste. The traitors will be exposed to an endless series of brutal jolts that will tear their flesh and break numerous bones in their bodies.

Henry has no doubt that they deserve their fate, but even he cannot help but feel pity for them. They could have avoided all of this. This is all very unfortunate.

Later, Henry joins the crowd at Tyburn. The execution has turned into a huge spectacle. Masses of people and horses are everywhere. In the centre are the scaffold with gallows, a large cauldron, and a fire. Next to the scaffold is a stand for the wealthier spectators and the nobility. Henry pushes through the crowd to get a good view of the executions as they unfold.

The four martyrs are brought to the scaffold, surrounded by guards. They have endured much already. Their robes are torn, and their faces and limbs look contorted and bloody. The shortest in the group grimaces in pain as he struggles to stand up straight and wobbles when forced to walk.

The first Carthusian to be taken to the scaffold is John Houghton. The hermit monk looks frail but devout. He starts to shake when he is on the scaffold and barely manages to give a short speech in honour of his German patron St Bruno. It is hard to hear him until he kneels and recites parts of Psalm 30. "…weeping may stay for the night, but rejoicing comes in the morning," the monk says with a hoarse voice. The furore in the crowd dies down. Henry, like everyone else, listens to the monk's final words respectfully.

After the monk stands, the hangman uncoils the free end of a rope and then tosses the rope to another man, who is positioned on the beam above. The man ties the rope firmly to the beam.

Next to the scaffold, the other monks pray while the preparations take place. Their voices are clear and strong, and many in the crowd join them in prayer.

It is uncomfortable for Henry to witness such unity in the crowd and to see the loyal support for these traitors. Even now, he feels anger that the monks refused to obey him, their king.

A moment later, Houghton stands on the scaffold with the rope around his neck and looks at all those in front of him. There is no fear in the man's eyes. He is ready to die.

The hangman directs the monk up the ladder. When he is a few steps up, the hangman acts swiftly, pushing the monk off the ladder. The monk's body swings through the air, tightening the rope around his neck. Houghton's face turns blue, and he gags as he tries to breathe, but the ordeal does not end there.

The hangman cuts Houghton loose, and his body falls to the ground. Semiconscious, they drag him away and lay him on a nearby table. They strip Houghton of his habit. Naked and dazed, he lies there. Then the executioner slits his chest open, and the poor devil releases his last breath.

The executioner first takes out Houghton's heart. His intestines are next, and then he cuts off his private parts. All of it is thrown into the nearby fire. Lastly, they cut off his head and hack the rest of the body into quarters. These four parts will be hung in different parts of London.

One after the other, all the monks undergo the same bloody fate. The last to be taken to the scaffold, which is splattered with blood by that point, is the Bridgettine. Henry recognises him now as the monk who accompanied him at Syon Abbey and saved him from the fire. He is Richard Reynolds, the confessor priest.

Reynolds never stopped praying aloud during the executions of his brothers. Now that it's his turn, he is calm and dignified. This impresses the crowd. Henry knows that many of them sympathise with Reynolds' cause.

"Though he shall have a sharp dinner, I trust in Jesus Christ he shall have a most sweet supper," one of his admirers in the crowd says.

Henry wishes he could deny this, but even he knows it is true.

Henry had instructed for Reynolds' head to be mounted at the abbey's gate as an example for all the others. While he thinks about this, he realises an important truth.

Henry is no longer at Tyburn or surrounded by fire. He is back on the cliff, looking down at the valley below.

"There's always hope for a new life, a new beginning," A voice behind him says.

Reynolds steps forward and turns to Henry. His glazed-over eye, the many scars, and the lesions on his neck are all there. Henry stares at him for a few seconds, absorbing all the horrific details of his face.

"Why do you walk around like that?" Henry asks.

Reynolds chuckles. "I'm proud of these scars," he says, touching his neck and face. "God has seen fit to reward me for my faith. A future pope will make me a martyr. I'll be a saint one day." Reynolds says it without sarcasm or bitterness.

The effect this has on Henry is profound. He wants to scold Reynolds and joke that he is surprised that there will be popes in the future, but he holds back because of his newfound respect for the man. Then he decides to defend himself.

"Public executions, as barbaric as they may be, weren't invented by me. They've been an integral part of English life since medieval times to protect the law of the country. Not that I think there should've been less of them. On the contrary, there should've been more. You, of all people, should know that the king is God's servant for your good. If you do wrong, be afraid, for he does not carry the sword in vain," Henry says, quoting the Bible.

Reynolds could have responded with an equally powerful citation, but he doesn't. Instead, he takes a different approach.

"They were good people," Reynolds says, referring to the many brothers who were executed. "William Exmew and I studied together at Cambridge, and I was proud to call him my friend. He enlightened my life in so many ways. After his studies, he went on to become a Carthusian hermit, and despite his young age, he was a man of great prestige."

As far as Henry is concerned, Exmew was stubborn and foolish, a danger to the Reformation and the country.

"They forced him to stand upright for fourteen days in chains with iron rings around his neck, hands and feet, bound to a post," Reynolds continues, "before he was hanged, drawn and quartered at Tyburn. He was a humble soul and a devout servant of God who lived a life of silence and contemplation in the monastery."

This is the first time Henry detects strong emotions in the monk's voice.

"They tried everything, but they couldn't break him. He stayed true to his faith."

With unease, Henry listens to Reynolds and decides he will not be drawn into a debate about something that will serve no purpose and no one at this point.

"He could have lived and spared himself his misery," Henry replies. "That's all I have to say about it." He turns his back to Reynolds and starts to walk away.

"I knew all of them, the Carthusian martyrs," Reynolds says. The monk's choice of the word "martyr" disturbs Henry, but he will not take the bait.

"Don John Houghton from the London Charterhouse, and Robert Lawrence and Augustine Webster, I knew them personally," Reynolds says. "Besides them, I met Sebastian Newdigate several times."

The mountains and hills in front of Henry are coloured a deep red. They look like a desert at sunset. Henry looks at them, lost in thought. He knew Newdigate as well. Sebastian was a close friend. Before he became a hermit monk at the London Charterhouse, he was part of the court and the privy chamber.

Newdigate was charismatic and witty and had a natural authority and warmth. Henry enjoyed his company and admired him even when he withdrew from public life and took up the cross. It was hard for Henry to accept that someone like Newdigate refused to acknowledge him as the supreme head of the Church.

"Newdigate was a good man," Henry says.

The monk looks up with curiosity at Henry. "They say that while he stood in chains in his cell in Marshalsea, Jesus visited him during the night. Not once but on several occasions."

Henry is flabbergasted. "The only person who visited him there was me," he says angrily. "It wasn't Jesus who came to see him. I went there incognito to see my friend and tried to talk some sense into the man."

Henry visited him twice, as a matter of fact, first in Marshalsea and then in the Tower. He was shocked to see his emaciated friend in his cell. Both times Henry offered Newdigate wealth and privilege if he would cave in, and both times Newdigate refused. As a result, he was hanged, drawn and quartered at Tyburn in June of the same year, just like the others.

"The stench in his cell was repellent," Henry says. "When I left, I instructed the guards to clean it."

Reynolds ignores Henry. Instead, he recounts the story as he believes it happened. "Sebastian was exhausted. He had cramps and pains all over his body. The pain was excruciating. Thoughts raged through his head like a storm until, suddenly, *He* came to him, Jesus Himself. Jesus stood in front of him. He smiled at him. His love was strong and wonderful, and in His hand was a key. He told Sebastian that with that key, He would unchain him and set him free."

Henry shakes his head. "It wasn't Jesus who came to see him. It was I who stood in front of him and held a key in my hand. It was me who offered him his freedom."

Without anger, Reynolds looks at Henry in search of any signs of guilt or remorse for what he did to him and his brothers in Christ. Through his one good eye, he doesn't see any such thing.

"It was Jesus," Reynolds says, smiling softly. "From then onwards, Sebastian knew that Jesus would be waiting for him in Paradise. That was the freedom He spoke about."

Henry does not want to hear it. He wants to object, but the monk takes a few steps back, then turns and walks away.

CHAPTER NINETEEN
THE DARK KNIGHT

THE NIGHT IS SHROUDED in mist, provoking a sense of mystery and foreboding. Hidden at the cliff's edge is a steep staircase made from limestone. The endless steps going down are slippery and reach far and deep.

As a young prince, Henry was brought up with the romance and ideals of chivalry. King Arthur and the mystique surrounding the Knights of the Round Table were important in his life and that of his father, both of them drawing inspiration from such tales. Could this twilight world be Henry's Avalon? Will he find his healing and peace here? It may well be, and somehow it makes sense to him as he starts to descend the stairs.

Accompanied by the hoot of an owl and the croaking of frogs, he reaches the bottom. Hidden in the mist, not far from him, a large animal snorts. Henry stands still and listens. It is a black morel horse. The animal is tall and strong, and his mane and tail are long and silky.

It is a stallion, and Henry can tell when he approaches the horse that it has a responsive and fiery character. Henry smiles. It's just how he likes his horses to be.

The remarkable beast is saddled and bridled like a courser. That is interesting. It is a horse ready for battle, and it stands with pride and confidence before him. Henry looks around to see if his master is nearby, but no one is there.

On the ground next to the horse are pieces of iron armour. There is also a halberd and a spear with an axe mounted on it.

What is all this doing here? Could this be an invitation to fight? Curious, he looks up toward the horse.

"Calm down," he says quietly. The horse neighs in return. "Good horse," Henry says as he walks up to it and pats it while admiring its strength. "Good boy," he whispers. The horse relaxes in response to his soothing voice.

The armour on the ground is a chest plate. Henry picks it up and studies it. It has a good weight, and the details etched into it are unique and intricate. He admires the exquisite craftsmanship. The engraving of the Tudor Rose on the chest enthrals him. He has never seen anything like it, not even in the workshop of the Greenwich armoury or in Europe.

As he inspects the armour further, it strikes him that it will likely fit him. It is only natural to try it on, and it is a perfect fit. This pleases him. Out of habit, he poses as if an audience is watching and admiring him. He smiles. This is familiar territory for him. He kneels and grabs the halberd. It is heavy and handsomely made. The pike and the axe are both sharp. When he touches the axe with his finger, he cuts himself, and blood drips.

"Blast!" he yells, putting his bloody finger into his mouth to soothe it.

"No helmet?" he whispers. The horse snorts in response. The fact that there is no helmet makes Henry's heart race. Whoever left the armour here made it clear it was not for make-believe or a show fight. You do not fight in a tournament or a friendly battle with a weapon as sharp and as lethal as this without a helmet. It would be a slaughter if he were alive. This is an invitation for real combat, serious warfare, but with whom?

As a young man, he was the best jouster in the country and was always on the lookout for a worthy opponent.

"The king has promised never to joust again except with a man as good as himself," he said in 1516 after a disappointing tournament. Only in Charles Brandon did he find someone he could respect as an opponent, and the two became best friends.

In life, he would have refused to enter a tournament with a halberd instead of a lance. It was never about killing his rival. The excitement of it all lay in the many rules of jousting and the complicated scoring structure. Even so, he feels exhilarated by this perilous prospect. It is as if he is young again, ready to take on the challenge and beat any adversary.

"A knight doesn't fear death," Henry whispers in the horse's ear. "A knight only fears living without courage." Then, without hesitation, he mounts the horse with confidence.

The horse jitters. Henry can tell it is uncomfortable with him and resisting him. Being familiar with horses, he tries to reassure the stallion and gently talks to him. This works well, and the horse calms down.

"Good boy," Henry says, and the horse trots forward onto the open square that lies in front of him.

Alert, he listens to any approaching sound and looks around him. Is anyone or anything here? Suddenly, the hairs on the back of his neck prick up. There may not be any signs of an opponent at this minute, but Henry is certain someone could show up soon. He spurs the horse on and canters toward the far end of the large open space.

Indeed, in the distance, almost invisible to the naked eye, he sees a knight on his horse. Henry reins in the horse and observes the mysterious rider coming toward him.

The knight's armour covers his body from top to bottom so he is less vulnerable than Henry. It does not intimidate Henry, but it seems unfair that the knight has much more protection. His armour includes a helmet enclosing his head to keep his skull and face safe. Most striking is that the helmet has ram horns protruding from it.

It is a devil's helmet and looks like a replica of the helmet that Henry received as a gift from the Holy Roman Emperor Maximilian I in 1514. This must be a sick joke. Whoever is wearing it must know about its significance. It is a provocation.

For an instant, Henry does not know how to take this, but he decides it will not deter him. On the contrary, he is determined to engage in battle, convinced he will defeat his opponent. His opponent is a coward to engage in an unequal fight.

Both stand still while facing each other, adversaries ready for war, a mere fifty metres between them. Calm as he is, Henry takes the situation in.

He has always been someone who has great focus when he engages in a demanding physical activity. It does not matter if it is a sport, a hunt or a jousting match. He has a natural ability to quiet himself and focus all of his attention on winning. It's just the way he is and always has been.

From the jousting tournaments he participated in, he knows that the mind of the horse and the rider become one in battle. A sublime unity emerges. The experience strangely excites him. He loves it when the tension builds. It requires skill to take time, have patience and focus completely on facing the unknown. To be in a space where nothing else matters, as if the whole world and all thinking have reached a standstill. A space of nothingness and complete clarity.

Without being able to explain it, he senses that the knight hiding inside the shadows of his armour is ready to make a move. It is only a matter of seconds now. Henry feels it. It is as if he can hear the knight's accelerated breathing and heartbeat.

And indeed, the horse and its rider step forward. Seconds later, both Henry and the knight are trotting toward each other. Headed for a bloody confrontation, they spur their horses on to a gallop. As they reach full speed, there is no turning back. Everything is set. Destiny awaits. It is Henry or the other. Live or die, if it is possible to die twice.

Henry aims for his opponent's head and neck, where the knight is most vulnerable.

The knight comes into full view, storming toward him from the darkness and mist. Henry's horse races at full speed. He balances the halberd and prepares to strike. They gallop toward each other until there are only a couple of metres between them. This is it. The moment he will strike.

At the last moment, the knight changes course and disappears. This is not what Henry expected. Where is he?

In Henry's world, there are rules and codes of conduct in chivalry. This is cunning and deceitful. There is no time to think it through. He needs to turn his horse around and prepare for the knight to approach him from the other side, but it is already too late. Before Henry can turn his horse around, a crushing blow hits his head. He loses his balance and falls off his horse.

His horse has been knocked down as well. It stumbles and falls on top of him. The weight of the horse crushes him. Henry groans in pain. Only with a lot of struggle does he free himself and crawl away, staggering to his feet.

Dazed, he looks around and then stumbles away. It is pointless, though. The knight has returned. Galloping toward him, he strikes Henry again. This time it is even more severe. Henry is punched right in the middle of his chest and smacked against the ground.

Panting, and with blood dripping from his head, he lies in the dirt, pelted by heavy rain. With his eyelids swollen and covered in blood, he can hardly see.

The triumphant knight looks down at Henry from his horse. Then he dismounts and walks toward him. When he is less than two metres away from Henry, he stops. Henry lies motionless on the ground in anticipation. With no strength left, he surrenders to whatever the knight will do next.

The knight puts his sword away and takes his helmet off. Then he walks over to Henry and leans forward to get a good look at him. Henry groans and lifts his head to get a better look at the knight.

The man leans toward him. He is of Henry's age and has fiery red hair and a beard. In fact, the man looks exactly like Henry. He is his mirror image.

The knight gazes at him without pity. There is no mercy or compassion in his eyes. Instead, a sardonic smirk appears on his face. "You fool!" he cries, laughing.

The knight's eyes turn red. They no longer resemble the eyes of a human being. His face is no longer Henry's either. It is not even a human face anymore. Instead, it is the face of a demon. Petrified, Henry instinctively recoils.

"Dear God, help me," he whispers.

A vortex of black energy shoots down from the sky. Everything starts to vibrate around Henry. The air pressure changes noticeably, and the ground starts to shake. A low humming sound comes with it. The vortex covers the entire sky. It encircles the demon knight and horse and both disintegrate into millions of minuscule fragments. The vortex sucks up all these tiny bits and swallows them into its profound and impenetrable darkness.

The entire spectacle lasts no more than a few seconds and is followed by hailstones as big as oranges falling onto the square. Then it is all gone, the raging storm and the vortex of darkness.

It is a strange sensation to be surrounded by such a threat at one moment and find it all gone a second later. Bewildered, Henry looks around him.

His horse is now standing not far from him. The halberd lies metres away. Blood has stained the ground. In pain, Henry crawls toward some cover under a tree. Exhausted, he lies down and immediately falls asleep.

When he wakes up, the horse is standing next to him. It is as if the horse has been waiting for him. When Henry sees the horse, he starts to cry. There is no loyalty, no love between humans, that compares to that from an animal.

"You know what I'll call you?" he asks. "Canicida. You remind me in so many ways of him."

Canicida was Henry's favourite horse, though he loved and favoured many horses throughout his life. Horses could provoke emotions in him on par with true love and devotion. In his relationship with horses, there was always honesty, generosity and loyalty for him and the horse.

They never betrayed him, unlike his friends and the women in his life. He would talk to them endlessly, and they would not reply. He would pat them, treat them with care, look after their diet and give them remedies when they were sick.

Even after they retired, he would visit his "old friends" in the stables and check up on them. They were as important or even dearer to him than his real friends, only less complicated. With his horses, he was not the king. He could be one with them and forget everything else.

Canicida was a nimble reddish-brown horse with a black mane, tail and lower legs. A true beauty. Gentle, intelligent, stronger and faster than any other horse, and a good communicator too. Canicida was a joy to ride and to be in the presence of, a real character.

"That's right. Canicida. That's your name," he says, standing next to the horse. "You're my horse now. We belong together." The horse whinnies as if he understands. Henry inspects Canicida. He looks fine despite the fall earlier.

"You're strong, aren't you?" Henry whispers.

The moment has come to mount Canicida again. Henry is struggling. His whole body aches. It is a challenge, but the horse's patience is touching.

"Not so fast," a man says. A group of soldiers surrounds Henry. He recognises their uniforms. They are men from his own army, but before he can command them, one of the men knocks Henry to the ground.

CHAPTER TWENTY
JUDGMENT DAY

WHEN HENRY REGAINS CONSCIOUSNESS, he finds he is chained up like a caged animal, a linen sack over his head. His clothes are soaking wet, and it feels like someone has put a dagger through his gut and ripped out his intestines. It's hardly as bad as being unhorsed in a jousting tournament, but the pain is intense, and he moans in agony. Wherever he is, it's not very welcoming.

He tries to focus on the rhythm of the falling drops of water around him, but it is hard when his whole body aches and when he feels defeated and short-changed.

Approaching footsteps put him on alert. He can tell the soldiers are back. One of the men approaches him.

"Take him," a different soldier, positioned further away, orders.

Hands grab Henry and force him to get up. He lets out a groan of pain as he is pushed and freed from the chains around his ankles and wrists.

"This one's a real bastard," the man says, poking Henry in the ribs to get him moving. Henry screams in anguish. The soldiers snigger with contempt.

This is war, and Henry knows it. Perhaps not in the conventional sense, but the situation is deadly serious. His soul is at stake. Someone opposes him with a real vengeance. It is not God or his parents. He does not know who is plotting and scheming against him, but he knows this force is real and evil.

Who or what drives this force? It is most likely someone whose ambition for power was frustrated by Henry's authority. Someone who takes his chance in the umbra of this world.

The guard pushes forward and pokes him in the ribs with a blunt instrument. Henry screams in pain as he drags his injured leg in compliance. The man warns him that if he doesn't walk, he will throw him back on the ground and force him to crawl through the mud.

Henry does as he is told. Although hindered by the darkness, he shuffles forward as quickly as possible.

"Wait." One of the more senior soldiers orders them to stop. They have left the waiting cell where he was being held, and much more light comes through the linen sack over his head. The soldier comes toward them.

"Get him ready," he says. The man yanks the sack from Henry's head. The bright light blinds him. Where is he? The soldier does not give him much respite and orders him to keep walking.

Henry struggles to see where he is going. After a while, he can see more clearly. It looks like they are in a large hall. Everything is white, and from the murmur around him, he can tell a crowd is awaiting his arrival.

The hall is made of white marble, and Henry recognises it as the same hall he saw in his trance when he was on top of the cliff. The space is filled with benches made of hard pale wood. Its roof is crystalline in structure. It is a magnificent and astonishing design. It is all of a calibre he is not familiar with.

A cacophony of women sings praises to God. Their angelic voices reverberate around the hall. Just like in the dream, they are all dressed in white gowns.

In the front row sit Catherine of Aragon, Catherine Howard and Jane Seymour, three of his six wives. But there is an empty place. The remaining spot is missing its queen. What about Anne Boleyn? Where is she?

For a moment, Jane turns around, and just as in his earlier trance, she looks horrified to see him there and quickly turns back. She whispers something to Catherine of Aragon, who acknowledges it, but her response is one of expectation rather than surprise.

Behind his wives, there are many other women he knows, but also many he has never seen before. Some of them are from far-away countries, the colour of their skin much darker than anything he has seen before.

What is going on here? Why only women? He is led to a holding area and is forced to stand. He feels humiliated standing there half-naked, wounded and covered in dirt and blood. His clothing is torn and ragged, and his unruly hair and beard are unbefitting of his status.

He wants to raise his voice and claim his authority, show them who he is, but when he opens his mouth, no sound comes out. The chains around his ankles limit his movement and reduce him to a voiceless criminal without rights, vulnerable to abuse and mockery.

Twelve nuns in white habits enter the hall. They display serenity and modesty but also beauty and strength. A young woman, pretty and charismatic, walks in front of the group of twelve women. Straight away, he recognises her: Elizabeth Barton, the "Mad Maid" from Kent, as some call her. This certainly does not bode well for him.

Elizabeth, who is attractive with an air of innocence, takes her place in the centre of the hall. The singing stops, and it appears she will address the women who are present and, in particular, the three queens in the front row. The twelve nuns who accompany Elizabeth take their place behind her, probably to make it look more theatrical or spectacular.

"Dear ladies, welcome," she starts. "My name is Elizabeth Barton. I'm not here because I'm a scholar. I'm here as a woman from a humble and honest family. I'm devoted to God, the Virgin Mary and the Divine Feminine and have been asked to oversee these proceedings."

Henry fears this woman. He always did. She cannot be trusted. He feels she has the power to destroy him.

"Some of you have met me, while others have merely heard about me. I lived as a devout nun inside the holy tradition of the Roman Catholic Church. Most of you know me as the nun who had visions and revelations and could hear the voice of God and the Virgin Mary directly.

"I'll begin by presenting the bill of attainder against Henry
Tudor. The bill sets out that he lived as an immoral human being.
Three of his wives here with us will either approve or reject the bill
through a majority rule. They are all well-informed and briefed on
the matter. If they agree to the bill, it will authorise punishment,
the judgment being that Henry Tudor will not be allowed access
to the heavenly realms and will have to prepare for eternal life
without peace until he has proven otherwise."

What is she rambling on about? A bill of attainder against him?
The king? Henry shakes his head in despair. What a shambolic
and disastrous state of affairs.

"For those who wonder if I'm here because I seek revenge for
the king's cruelty toward me, I want to say the following," Barton
speaks clearly and confidently, but Henry has lost interest in this
theatre. He knows her story - how she had true premonitions and
visions. She's a lunatic, a self-proclaimed witch. He couldn't care
less about what she has to say.

Though half-naked and covered with dried blood and filth, he
no longer feels ashamed. His three wives, the queens, should be
embarrassed to allow this travesty. Tears fill his angry eyes. He does
not deserve this. How dare they judge him and allow their king to
be treated this way? Who is behind all of this?

In his mind, different scenarios present themselves. Is this
Anne's work? But Anne is nowhere to be seen. Maybe it's
Catherine's, his first wife?

He hardly dares to look at the three women he once knew
intimately. They sit still and upright in the front row, like Grecian
goddesses in their white gowns, but none smile or show any
compassion or affection toward him. They all ignore him. It feels
like a betrayal, a dagger to his heart, especially from his beloved
Jane. Why does she not stand up and tell them that her husband
cannot be treated this way?

"We're either a force for good or a force for evil. It's our choice,"
Barton says. Everybody applauds her as if she just spoke the
deepest of truths.

"Do I seek revenge?" she continues, returning to the issue of her
motive. "No, although I have ample reasons for it. Without a trial,
I was hanged, and my head was put on a pike on London Bridge.

But I don't just blame the king alone for it. I've always hoped I could save his dark, twisted soul. It was the learned men he relied on. I feared them as much or even more, especially Cromwell. He screamed and yelled at me when I was brought before him. He was terrifying, a bully. Cranmer, who interviewed me as well, was very different. He behaved civilly and feigned compassion. Personally, I thought he was an idiot. I didn't respect him as a man of the highest calling. Only when it suited him. He was like an accountant." Henry has to give her that. "He would write everything down even when I sighed or paused; he would write down: 'sigh' or 'pause.'"

The women in the audience laugh. Elizabeth looks embarrassed.

"That was the Elizabeth Barton of the past talking again," she says with a hint of irony, then smiles apologetically. "We're all easy prey for the forces of evil."

CHAPTER TWENTY-ONE
THE WIVES

JANE SEYMOUR, Henry's third wife and the one to whom he was most loyal, rises from her seat reluctantly. He immediately recognises her reservation about speaking in public. She is so lovely and such a gentle soul. He was blessed to have her on his side for a time. Looking at her now, he chokes back his tears.

Slowly, she walks over to the podium, where she will address the women who are present. Her white dress is embroidered with delicate silk flowers. It is pleasantly simple and devout. She wears neither jewellery nor a headdress. Her blonde hair hangs loose over her delicate shoulders.

She looks sideways to where Henry stands. Despite his chains and his miserable appearance, she nods briefly. It is a simple gesture, but means the world to him, and a strong, warm feeling fills him. It has been a long time since he felt like that.

He remembers her as a good woman, strong when she felt she could be and docile when needed. Many would say she is not very attractive, but he always thought she had beauty, and he desired her. She was aloof and distant yet always interested in being intimate and loving. Her love for him was constant and genuine. She was always loyal to him. He knows that for certain. She will speak in his favour. He is sure of it.

Jane takes her place on the podium and looks at the women in front of her. Then she clears her throat and starts to speak. "Dear ladies, I feel honoured and privileged to stand in front of so many gifted, beautiful and prestigious women. Among you, of course, is my beloved Queen Catherine, whom I served as a maid-of-honour." She looks in Catherine's direction.

"She is someone I admire and revere. I have good memories of my time in service to her. She was like a mother and a confidante to me, one of the few people in my life who understood me as a person and woman. Together, she and I shared much affection and laughter. She was also my inspiration when I adopted my motto, 'Bound to obey and serve,' during my time as queen consort. I have always believed that in service, we find our bliss, and through this perspective, I will judge the bill."

She pauses to catch her breath before continuing. "It's not and never has been my intention to place myself as the judge to review the life of anyone and their readiness for the heavenly realms. I certainly wouldn't like to do that now with my former husband. I have to say that after reviewing all the important men in my life, I've concluded that they were all intoxicated by their desire for power—my father, my brothers and certainly also my husband. None of them was kind or genuine in his affections. They all left it to us women to love, be kind and be forgiving." She stops again and hesitates.

"I regret to say that when they asked my husband during the complications of the birth of our son if they should let me or our child live, my husband, without any hesitation, readily answered that it was the child's life that should be saved and not that of his wife. My husband never saw me as a person with a value apart from himself. I was there for only one reason: to please him and give him a son.

"So, after careful consideration, I leave it to God to make this call, but in my humble opinion of someone who loved him, he is not yet ready or qualified to be in heaven. Therefore, I agree with the bill's contents and the judgment laid out before him."

Her words are a blow to Henry. He cannot believe what he has just heard. Are these her own true thoughts? It cannot be. Someone must have forced her to say them. This is not the Jane who was his queen.

Jane returns to her seat. The hall is quiet. No applause or murmurs.

Catherine Howard climbs the podium. Petite and beautiful, she is wearing a white satin dress with white pearls and rings with translucent rubies. Her hair is tied up. She is elegant, relaxed, confident, and comfortable presenting herself to a larger audience.

"My dear ladies, I feel honoured and humbled to be asked to speak in front of so many talented women. I promise you I will be brief. What I have to say is very simple, but before I do, let me tell you a little about the circumstances that led me to become His Majesty's wife. How I was introduced to adult life as a woman." Catherine pauses and clenches her hands for a moment before she continues.

"When I was a happy, innocent young girl, my music teacher, Henry Maddox, whom I admired for his talent and seniority, molested me." She chokes back her tears as she recalls the devastation she had experienced.

Catherine stops to look at the women in the front few rows to gauge their reactions. She knows many of them will empathise. They look genuinely shocked and taken back by her frank admission.

"It started in an innocent, almost playful way. He would lay his hand on my shoulder, arm and waist. He would lean forward, and I would feel his breath against my ear and cheek. He would compliment me. First, subtle and charming, later rudely and obnoxiously. I didn't ask him to do this, nor did I encourage him. Instead, I made it clear that I didn't enjoy his attention." She stops for a moment and looks at her audience.

"Still, I had no idea what was to come next. One afternoon when I arrived for my lesson, he was very different. He didn't seem himself, and he avoided eye contact with me. I wondered what was going on until he grabbed me and pushed me against the wall, forcing himself on me. I remember his angry face very close to me. He grunted and panted. It was awful. My mind went blank. I left my body for a while, until it was over. I was thirteen at the time and in the company of a man entrusted with my care. This was my first encounter with how men can behave toward women." She stops again. Her hand trembles slightly, and there is a twitch of her lips.

"I don't hate men, but men in power are often predators. They feel they own you, that you're their toy and exist merely for their pleasure. Let me tell you this: I am opposed to predators and those abusing their power." She pauses as the women in the audience applaud her. "I believe in mutual respect and freedom. Very rarely are men condemned for their behaviour toward women, yet many have criticised me for my actions. They told me I'm selfish and even… a whore." She pauses for a moment, clearly upset.

"It was not I who was delusional. It was this man here." She points at Henry. All eyes turn to him. "He mistook lust for love. He ordered it as he ordered good wine or venison for dinner. Together with his machinery of power and the many men who served him, he has corrupted and stained his entire reign. There were no heroes in my life, no knights who came to my rescue. I was seventeen when the king chose me as his bride. He was forty-nine, obese and, quite frankly, a grotesque, sick man, old enough to be my father. He was a monster, and he behaved like one. Without a shadow of a doubt, the bill of attainder is correct and should be enforced."

She remains at the podium as if there is more she wants to say. Everybody looks at her. What else is she going to do?

"It was Francis Dereham whom I truly loved. Him and no one else. He is the only man I truly married."

"Tell us more about him." One of the women cries out.

Catherine is hesitant to do so, but the other women are curious too. She smiles. "Let me tell you a true story of love."

The silly girl just publicly confessed to the crimes she was accused of in 1542. Henry is disgusted and does not want to listen to her story of love. He looks at Catherine of Aragon. She must be horrified as well. The frivolity of this girl. Her sheer stupidity. Why did he make her a queen consort of England? She's an embarrassment.

Catherine tells the story of her love for Francis Dereham and how their relationship was true and special. While she does this, Henry stares at her pale face and her eyes. She looks stubborn and yet vulnerable. A strange lust rises in Henry. It was always there when he was with her, a will to have her and force her to be his. The feeling embarrasses him now. Why does he feel so provoked by her? The question preoccupies him, and he does not hear a word of the rest of Catherine's speech, only becoming aware of her again when she thanks the audience for listening to her story.

Catherine of Aragon is the last queen to address the hall. Her white dress is made of a rough linen compared to the others. Her auburn hair is loose and rests on her shoulders. She looks young and beautiful. For Henry, it does not make that much difference.

She carries a small book with her. It has a Tudor rose on the cover and *fleur-de-lis* patterns. She opens it when she is on the podium and starts to read a passage from it.

"Sisters, this day is the end of our slavery and the beginning of our freedom, the end of sadness, the source of joy, for this day consecrates a young man who is the everlasting glory of our time and makes him your king, a king who is worthy not merely to govern a single people but singly to rule the whole world. Such a king as him will wipe the tears from every eye and put joy in the place of our long distress. Every heart smiles to see its cares dispelled, as the day shines brightly when clouds are scattered. Now the people, freed, run before their king with bright faces. Their joy is almost beyond comprehension. They rejoice, they exult, they leap for joy and celebrate their having such a king. 'The king' is all that any mouth can say." She closes the book and looks up at the women in front of her.

"Thomas More wrote these words to commemorate our coronation at Westminster Abbey on June 24, 1509. It was midsummer's day and the feast of St John the Baptist. This ode was not a random choice of words. We all felt them in our hearts. The joy, the excitement and the hope, described so well by More, were real and palpable throughout the kingdom. It's hard now to imagine the energy and charisma that my young husband possessed during these early years. I've often wondered what drove him to destroy the hope and the promise he so clearly carried within him and to end up such a disappointment in every possible way. It has maddened me, but I know it's not my task to solve the riddle of his tormented soul. He, and he alone, will have to face God and ask for forgiveness.

"For me, as I have explained at length on previous occasions, I simply cannot see how there can be a passage to heaven for a man who has treated his wives and family so deceitfully. It has destroyed all of us, including him. But now I'm free of him, and he's no longer my concern. I cannot be his judge or save him from his misdemeanours. I underwrite the bill, but more importantly, I trust that God, in all His wisdom, will ultimately decide the destination of his soul's journey."

Henry feels pain throughout his body. Catherine's words are harsh and unnecessarily brutal. He takes it as only a man can take adversity. He endures it and waits for it to pass.

Until now, Henry has observed the whole process quietly. The scale of the event under the large glass dome has affected him deeply.

Naturally, he feels humiliated, wronged and misunderstood. He wishes he could tell his side of the story to explain to these women the real world of power. They have no idea. They judge him without being able to see. What about justice?

Also, all three women did not show any reservations toward him while they were alone. Catherine Howard was, despite her objections, very affectionate and even enthusiastic toward him in bed. Only Catherine of Aragon would tease him at times and make him feel he was a naughty boy whom she had to educate and instruct. She was older than him by several years, so that was understandable.

His disappointment is mostly focused on Jane. He had hoped to reunite with her. She belongs by his side as his queen, or at least that is what he thought.

He is relieved that Anne was not present. There was no mention of her, which is odd given her presence at the trial. Not that her contribution would have made things any better. On the contrary.

Elizabeth Barton returns to the stage. All three wives have returned to their seats. It looks like she is about to make a big announcement.

"We're all threads in a beautiful tapestry that brings us here together. Mothers, sisters, daughters, friends. Love to you all," she says.

Henry expects more will be said, but instead, trumpets sound from the different corners inside the dome, spectacularly filling the air.

Despite his reservations about the trial, he is moved by the sheer excitement of the remarkable scene that follows. Beautiful winged luminescent angels become visible and sweep down from the sky above. The beings illuminate the entire dome. At the same time, the dome starts to slide open, and rays of light flood the hall. What architecture. What a construction. The source of the light is a mystery, but it is majestic and resonates with a frequency of pure love that can be felt tangibly.

A multitude of angels flies over the heads of the women, and a cacophony of cheers and gasps of awe greet them. There is laughter and shrieks of joy as the angels dive and soar over the crowd.

There is one larger angel. It stands next to Elizabeth Barton and Catherine Howard. Its wings are enormous, and its light shines most brilliantly. Its face is gentle and serene, and for an instant, Henry can tell it is looking at him. It makes him feel humble and shy. It is so strong in its love.

The angel lifts the two women. Together they fly through the air toward the opening in the dome and disappear into the sky beyond.

Jane is next, followed by all the other women that are present. Each of them is accompanied by their own personal angel. Henry is flabbergasted and stands in shock at what is taking place.

The last one who departs is an angel with a golden glow. This angel carries Catherine of Aragon. He observes how this last angel lifts her and carries her out of sight.

The afterglow of the angels' light lingers in the hall, but after a while, the feeling of euphoria fades, and the entire glass dome that was once translucent and alive, bit by bit, disappears along with everything in it.

A guard grabs Henry from behind while another pulls a sack over his head. These must be the soldiers who have come to collect him. They punch him and push him forward. He stumbles and almost trips over the heavy iron chains around his ankles. They lead him down some granite stairs into the damp, sinister hallway of an underworldly prison.

CHAPTER TWENTY-TWO
KEPT IN THE DARK

HENRY LIES COILED in a heap on the stone floor, surrounded by dirt and debris. The floor is wet and cold. When he asked them where he was, one of the guards laughed and said, "Pride before the fall."

They kicked him in the stomach one last time before they left. He can still hear their footsteps in the distance as they walk away.

When it is quiet, he lifts himself and removes the sack they pulled over his head. He gasps for air. It is pitch dark in the cell. Only through an iron gate is there a glimmer of light from the outside world. A curious variety of muffled voices comes from nearby. Some whisper, and others moan in hopeless desperation.

Henry picks himself up off the floor and groans from the pain of his bruised ribs. Is he alone in the cell? He suspects not. The pungent smell of rotting flesh is nearby, making him nauseous.

His first instinct is to walk toward the gate to see if it is locked, but he bumps into something in the dark. He reaches out to touch a tall, wooden pole. It feels wet.

As he slides his hand farther along the pole, he feels the contours of an old man's face. Horrified, he pulls his hand back. "Who are you?" he says with a commanding voice. There is no reply, no movement or any sound. He stretches his hand out again and feels a beard, lips and a nose. While he examines the face with his fingers, he realises the head has been severed from its body and is sitting on a spike.

It repulses him, and he shuffles backwards, only to discover he is surrounded by more of the same hidden in the darkness. Each spike carries its own bloody figurehead. He pushes past them to get to the gate and the flicker of light beyond, but in his determination to get away, he runs into a spike, and the head of a bald middle-aged man topples onto the floor with a loud thud.

Behind the gate lies a hallway. As far as Henry can tell, he is in a vast underground dungeon with many cells just like his. At the far end of the hallway and out of sight, there must be a fire. The shadow of its flames dances on the wall.

Henry clutches the gate and tries to shake it open, but it doesn't move at all. At that moment, he notices the bloodstains on his hands and wipes them against the tattered remains of his hose. What a sad state of affairs this is.

Despite the darkness, he can make out a man's outline in the opposite cell.

"Have you seen it?" the man asks. "The hellish fire of the pit?"

The hellish fire? Henry does not know how to respond. The man stumbles closer to the gate of his cell. He is older-looking, and two of his front teeth are missing. His scrawny, partially naked body is covered in filth and bloodstained. He gestures to Henry, his eyes full of fear. "It says in the Bible that they shall cast them into a furnace of fire," the man hisses, "that there shall be wailing and gnashing of teeth."

It disturbs Henry, and he remembers what the guard said earlier. As he looks down the hallway, there are more men like this fellow. A few of the prisoners sit quietly and alone. Some have lost their minds. They talk to themselves and make wild gestures with their arms as if fighting off an invisible intruder. Others whisper to their neighbours, afraid of being detected. They all stop what they are doing when they become aware of Henry.

"Don't believe a word he says," a bearded prisoner with a well-spoken accent says. "I've studied the reflection of those lights on the wall." The man points in the direction of the reflection. He could be a scholar or might have been one at one time. "When there is a lot of movement on the wall, the flames outside must climb higher, just as they are now. I know what it means," he continues. "There's a logic to them, and this is the first time they've gone up as high as this. It's a sign."

"You don't want to see the truth for what it is," Henry's gloomy, apocalyptic neighbour says. "If you would be quiet for a moment, you would hear the lamentations of those poor souls burning in hell."

Henry nods. His neighbour is right. In the distance, the faint sound of wailing voices can be heard periodically. Henry did not notice it before. It has an eerie quality.

The scholar, nevertheless, insists that it is nonsense and that the opposite is true. "Someone will come, and we will all be set free. I know it for certain."

The exchange between the two men seems to be part of some daily ritual. After the scholar and his neighbour have spoken their piece, all the men return to what they were doing in their cells. Even Henry's neighbour withdrawals into a dark corner of his cell.

For hours nothing changes. He is seated on the floor and watches the reflection of the flames dance on the prison wall. He studies it carefully in an attempt to understand its significance.

He is initially reluctant, but must agree with his neighbour that it is likely a reflection of a big fire outside the prison wall. Nevertheless, he finds that staring at it soothes him, and for a while, he manages to forget the confines of his cell as his mind is transported back to his youth.

His father had been taken ill, and there was concern he did not have long to live anymore. Henry found him distressed and defeated on his knees in his bedchamber, lost in his own world.

An astute Henry saved the situation by reciting the words of Psalm 17: "And I called upon the Lord in my distress, and from His Holy Temple He heard my voice."

His father looked surprised at first. Did he not understand the meaning of the words? But after a while, the expression on his face changed. Henry's father smiled and looked as if God Himself had spoken to him.

Like his father, Henry has been on his knees for a while, and even though he does not feel God's presence, to pray for help feels like the right thing to do.

It is only after a long time, when all the joints in his body start to ache, that he gets up and stretches.

It is of no use, he decides. There is no epiphany or sense of communion. He is all by himself, alone, in prison. It had to come to this.

REPENTANCE

CHAPTER TWENTY-THREE
THE PILGRIM

HENRY, DUKE OF CORNWALL, visits his mother in the intimate drawing room of their residence. His mother wears her hair loose over her shoulders. It has turned completely white during her time spent in the upper realms of heaven. Her dress, made of coarse, raw silk, is cut in a delicate way around her figure.

His mother's face is pale, with no makeup or colouring on her lips or cheeks. Her blue eyes make a striking contrast to her pale complexion and white hair.

Young Henry looks at her, bemused. "You look like a wise woman." Catherine strokes her hair, and they both chuckle.

"You've changed too. You're a man now and very handsome," she says. "I'm proud of you, my angel."

"I have something for you," he says and offers her a book of Psalms. The psalter is in a binding of gold damask and has parchment leaves decorated with rich illuminations that tell Bible stories.

His mother studies it with delight. She thumbs through the pages. "It's wonderful," she says and looks at him. "I hope it's not a parting gift."

"You know it has to be this way," he replies, but she ignores his remark.

"I can see the disapproval in your eyes." He knows recent events still haunt her. His father, in the Court of Heaven, looked unrepentant and indignant. She tries to distract herself and turns toward the open windows to look out over the rolling hills beyond her Spanish castle, with its colourful banners of Aragon and Castile.

He can tell that despite the joy of being reunited with him and his siblings, the betrayal she experienced in her marriage and the turbulence that it caused his sister, Mary, who still lives on the earthly plain, continues to trouble her soul.

He decides to change the subject. "What is that?" he asks, pointing to a tiny brooch pinned to her dress.

She grasps the gold scallop shell between her fingers. "It's the emblem of St James. It was given to me by a pilgrim I once met in Santiago de Compostela. Pilgrims who undertake the Camino wear it as a sign of their devotion to God and for protection on their journey."

Henry smiles. His mother never told him the story. "I didn't know this," he says with love in his voice. "When did this happen?"

His mother gives him a searching look, then gestures for him to sit next to her. "I was fifteen years of age when I visited the cathedral in the town on my way to England to marry your father's brother, Arthur. Something compelled me to talk to an elderly pilgrim in the congregation. His face radiated with peace, and I was curious to know if he had found God. He told me how he had started on his journey with the same question."

Henry looks at her, eager to know the answer. It grieves him to think of his father alone in the wilderness.

"The pilgrim confided in me. When he started his pilgrimage, he hoped for a revelation, a vision of some sort. But instead, during his journey, he was preoccupied mostly with meaningless thoughts, everyday things like which path to take. The one alongside the hill or the one across it? He debated which items to keep in the cloth sack he carried and which to leave behind to lighten the load."

"Did he find God?"

"The pilgrim admitted that he didn't know for certain. He had been too busy with the painful blisters on the soles of his feet, the hunger in his belly and the cold, biting wind that chilled his bones."

"There must have been a time when God spoke to the pilgrim," Young Henry insists. "Perhaps when he reached a point of exhaustion and felt like giving up."

"There were moments, yes, but they were fleeting," she replies. "One morning, for instance, he sensed God's presence just after dawn, when high up in the mountains, he looked out over the valley below that was covered in fog. There was a time when he was hiding under a pine tree to take shelter from a storm. The sound of the raindrops falling around him brought him closer to God. But they were just moments. They didn't last."

"But they were moments of communion with God, nevertheless," Henry insists, feeling a light of hope in him.

His mother must sense this. "I can see that you understand what the pilgrim was talking about," she remarks, then waits a moment before she continues speaking. There is an emotion on her face that she only has when talking about something really important to her. "I told him I wanted to become a nun and go on a pilgrimage myself one day," she says, looking almost shy to admit it.

"He must have liked that."

His mother shakes her head. "No. He was alarmed by it. 'I have to warn you, My Lady,' he said. I didn't understand his concern. Did he think I was not physically strong enough or that a woman could not serve God equally to a man? But it wasn't that. He explained that not everybody finds it easy to be on their own for long periods. Some people get nervous, even paranoid. He warned me that it is at those moments that Satan will tempt you and torment you."

"Satan?" Young Henry looks concerned.

She nods. "He knows when you're vulnerable. He accuses you, attacks you when you're weak, sick, or in pain, and feeds on your fear."

"On one occasion late at night, the pilgrim was roused by a terrifying presence. 'It was like a strong force, like a wind that came from nowhere,' he told me. For a moment, he thought it was a hungry wolf looking for its next meal. But then he came face to face with the devil's sharp claws, serpent-like eyes, and pale, gruesome face. 'He seeks to destroy those who carry the light of

Christ within them, and you must fight him off with the sword of the Spirit,' he warned. After he had finished his tale, he gave me this brooch for protection. God bless his soul."

"Mother. Are you afraid of the devil?" he asks.

"No." Catherine is defiant. "What more can he do to me?" She smiles. "He can't hurt me now. Something else happened to me in Santiago while I was there," she concludes. "I believe it was an omen."

Catherine visited the cathedral to attend Sunday Mass with many pilgrims from all over Europe. It is customary for the botafumeiro, a giant incense burner inside the cathedral, to swing through the air at great speed. It is quite a striking spectacle. It often takes up to eight men to move it due to its great size and weight. During her visit, one of the ropes snapped, and the men lost control of the botafumeiro. The golden vessel flew through a stained-glass window and crash-landed outside the cathedral. Thankfully, nobody was hurt, but Catherine was shaken.

"I was sure it was a warning about my doomed marriage to Arthur, but the alliance between England and Spain could only occur through our marriage. I had no choice but to go through with it, and when he died, I was forced to marry your father. Despite this, I never gave up my heartfelt desire to become a bride of Christ."

"What do you mean?" Young Henry asks.

"During my life, I took the vows of the third order of Saint Francis. Now I seek to join the order of Saint Dominic. I have already taken the vows of poverty, chastity and obedience. I'll fast and spend periods in silence as he did and live without the richness I've been used to. I'll wear only clothes made from pure, natural fibres, and the music and songs I listen to will celebrate all creation. I shall devote my life to praising, blessing and preaching the Gospel. *Laudare, benedicere, praedicare.* But I'll always be there for my angels."

"I'm happy for you, mother." He knows this is what her soul needs to heal and find eternal peace.

CHAPTER TWENTY-FOUR
PEARLS OF WISDOM

IT IS A BRIGHT, SUNNY MORNING. Young Henry's mother is ready to depart for her pilgrimage to the higher dimensions of heaven and its inner sanctum. Only the most devout souls can survive the frequency of love and ecstasy found there.

Dressed in a white habit, she kisses each of her children goodbye at the foot of the stone staircase. To make light of the situation, she shares a story with them.

"Children. Did you know Saint Dominic was also born in Castile?" she asks. "He was from Caleruega. They say his mother could not conceive and went on a pilgrimage to the abbey in Silos. She had a vivid dream while there and dreamt that a dog had jumped from her womb. It was carrying a burning torch in its mouth, and it set fire to the world. After this visit, she got pregnant with Saint Dominic."

His mother turns to Young Henry. "I knew you would understand my need to do this. Please take good care of your brothers and sisters while I'm gone. It won't be for long," she says with affection. Her expression changes to that of a concerned mother. She pulls him aside, away from the others. "And what about your father?" she asks. "Has anything changed?"

"He prayed."

She seems shocked by his response. "But he has now been sentenced. Not one woman came forward to speak in his defence. There's nothing you can do for him now." There is a hint of bitterness in her voice. Young Henry is displeased.

"Do not concern yourself," he says nonchalantly. "I've talked things through with my teacher." He does not want to divulge any of the details.

She wants to probe the matter further, away from the other children. "Why don't we walk through the gardens before I leave?" Catherine says. "We will be alone there, and you can confide in me."

The park that belongs to the castle is filled with magnificent sculptures, fountains and flowerbeds of many different varieties and colours. They walk down a path lined with tall Italian cypress trees. Birdsong and the sweet scent of gardenias fill the air.

Young Henry was not schooled in the same way as an earthly prince. He was and is still taught by the Spirit, and his mother will learn this magical process over time.

When it speaks to him, there is no physical person present, nor does it use spoken words to activate Henry's awareness. Questions are answered in the blink of an eye. Sometimes an entire library of words, pictures, mathematical equations, colours, emotions and sounds can be accessed simultaneously. They vibrate together to tell a complete story. His mind can absorb the information without delay, and his inner knowing feels a subject's various nuances and layers of meaning. He can access all of it at any time, should he wish.

He stops for a moment and looks at his mother. He is uncertain if she will understand his motivation for helping his father. She has not supported his decision so far. Before he speaks, he puts his hand on his heart and listens to the still, quiet inner voice that speaks to him.

"My father is in Limbo. He's a prisoner of his anger and pride, though he doesn't know it. Lost and alone, he lacks clarity of where his true destiny lies. I decree it will not be in the pit. There is hope. He has kneeled before God and asked for help. You and I agreed that if this happened, I would be allowed to go out there and help him."

Her face tightens. "What did your teacher say?" She asks him again to find confirmation of her fear that this is a bad idea.

"The answer from my teacher came in a split second. There were three parts to it. The first answers the question, 'What and who is God?'"

His mother is surprised by the first part of the answer but seems keen to find out more. "How did your teacher explain it?"

"God is everything that exists," Young Henry says. "All the people, the plants, the trees, the stars in the sky and everything else that we can think of between heaven and earth. That includes you, me and also my father."

His mother contemplates his words as he continues to speak. "God is the entire creation and simultaneously the One, the 'something,' that creates it. As the Bible says, God is the Alpha and Omega, the First and Last, the Beginning and End."

"God is love," Catherine adds. "I felt it in my heart when I was a little girl, and it never faded. It has always been there within me."

The Spirit taught Henry that saying there is nothing or no God is illogical. "Nothing" cannot create "something" or cause "something" to happen. It is also unnatural, as it is in our nature to be a part of the whole and to be a result of it. "By denying God, we deny our true nature. This denial leads to fear. Fear for others, fear for oneself and fear of death."

"I understand that," Catherine says. "Sin separates us from God and divides us as people. It requires humility to know God. Those who think of themselves as more important won't be able to experience God. They are blind, and their hearts will be hardened to the truth. Like your father."

Young Henry is quick to respond. "Humility or virtue, on the other hand, will drive him to look for the whole we are part of. The whole as in community, family, humanity, the animal kingdom, nature and the universe. This sense of oneness lives in all of us. It wants us to share and to nurture."

Although resistant at first, Catherine agrees with all of this. Her face relaxes, and she is attentive and at ease.

"Its principle is the principle of peace," he continues. "The peace that is always within our intention when we face the world and address the other. With peace as our guiding principle, reason and faith come together. They become one and the same. As a result, there is unity in everything should we choose to see it, and its measure is peace."

"When I think about it, it's all so beautiful," she says. "What was the second part of the message?"

Young Henry places his hand on top of his mother's. He smiles tenderly at her. "In the next part of the message, my teacher revealed what happens when physical life ends. This miraculous 'something' of being in the physical world cannot become 'nothing,' but after death, will transform into 'something else.' This 'something else' is immaterial and cannot easily be understood. You could say it is the memory or the unique signature of who we once were and everything that sums up our lives. This 'something else' is a fractal of God. It is eternal and will live forever. It is like an afterglow embedded in the whole of 'something' that encompasses everything. Nothing is lost, and everything and everyone after death goes through a step-by-step process of blending with the whole."

"That's why I'm embarking on this pilgrimage," she says. "I want to prepare myself to be reunited with God. But what about helping your father? Won't you endanger your soul by entering his state of Limbo?"

"The third part of the message was a warning on what to expect when I join my father. There is a risk that any misdemeanour from him could lower my vibration in frequency to feel pain and suffering. His pain and suffering. I could then become trapped in that frequency."

"I'm concerned for that reason," she replies. "Your father isn't like you. Your soul is pure and full of love. His soul is full of darkness. It may be too much. The darkness could overwhelm you."

"My teacher told me to treat him as one would treat a disobedient child—firm but fair and with love—but never to trust him to do the right thing. Not even when he promises or swears he'll do so."

Catherine scoffs. "Your teacher knows him well. Don't go," she pleads. "Please don't go."

"I have to do this. Won't you give me your blessing?"

His mother looks very sad all of a sudden. "What's wrong?" he asks. "What are you thinking?"

"I'm thinking back to when you were born. It was New Year's Day, 1511. I longed to hold you in my arms, but the delivery was hard, and I was too weak. Even so, the days after you were born were the happiest of my life. You were such a beautiful baby."

"The announcement of the royal birth was a joyous occasion. It came less than two years after our marriage. Your father made jokes and drank far too much. Many celebrations were planned throughout the land, and the biggest jousting event was organised. He showed off to the crowd by doing all kinds of clever manoeuvres and dressage on his horse during the tournament."

Catherine sighs deeply. "It was the most precious time. Never again did I see your father so euphoric. It was extraordinary, almost decadent. We received an avalanche of congratulations. Lavish gifts came in from all over the world. King Louis the Twelfth of France, your godfather, sent us a cup made from solid gold and a fine gold salt."

Catherine falls silent for a moment. Tears well up in her eyes. "Your death was a great loss to us both. It was one of the hardest things we faced as a couple. It hardened his heart toward me. I don't want to feel I could lose you again."

"You won't. I promise I'll return to you and bring the family peace. Please give me your blessing."

Without saying anything, Catherine looks at him as if to give her consent. She is proud of her son's courage and extends her arms to him.

CHAPTER TWENTY-FIVE
HELP ARRIVES

CATHERINE WAS RIGHT. The month she died was the month that everything changed for Henry. She cursed him. That's what he starts to believe now.

To escape his mental anguish, he walks toward the gate, hoping that the other men's voices will calm him.

It is not them but the silhouette of a tall young man who draws his attention. None of the other prisoners notices his presence as he passes by. At first, Henry wonders if this is a guard returning to finish him off, but he needn't worry.

Despite the darkness of his surroundings, he recognises the lad. The same young man had stood in the courtroom beside Catherine, claiming to be his son.

In the court, Henry had only a brief moment to observe him. Now that he sees him again, he must admit their resemblance is uncanny. Unlike before, he no longer distrusts his identity. This is indeed his son. The one he longed for.

Everything about him—his handsome face, strong physique, and fearless demeanour—reminds Henry of what he once possessed, but such temporal things no longer matter to him. In this miserable place, the young man who stands before him, his son, embodies all that is good about human nature, and with him comes hope.

"Father, don't be afraid," the young man says with a tender voice.

Henry feels embarrassed. He wants to say something, but what? Their first encounter ended so badly. Henry had been taken by surprise at the trial and had felt overwhelmed by it all. Maybe the lad wants an apology. Luckily for him, the young man leads the way.

"I'm here to help free you from your past so that you may find peace." He sounds sincere.

"Did your mother send you?"

He shakes his head. "She didn't want me to come here."

Henry scoffs. "And why is that?"

The lad does not answer this question. He knows better than that.

Henry glances across to the opposite cell. Thankfully, the prisoner is nowhere to be seen. He is probably ensconced in a dark corner of his cell.

"So, you wish to set me free? It's true; I want to leave this place more than anything," Henry admits. "If you can arrange that for me, I gladly accept your offer of help."

"It can be arranged. On one condition."

"What is that?"

"Your freedom comes with responsibility. You must repent by making amends for all the harm you have caused."

There you have it. He wants an apology. His mother must have instructed him to get one. What other motive could he have for being here now?

"What difference would it make if I did the things you ask? What I did in the past. What has happened. Can any of it be undone?" Henry waits for an answer. Instead, his son extends his hands to him as if to reassure him that nothing is impossible.

This simple gesture touches Henry. He had been exposed to flattery, intrigue and lies his entire life. It had made him suspicious of everyone at court, and he questioned all expressions of affection. This time it feels different. Genuine. Real.

Without hesitation, he grabs his son's hands through the gate's bars. He does not say anything, he just clutches his son's hands and starts to tremble. The emotions are powerful, and he can tell the young lad feels them too. Both of them are moved by the intimacy of the moment.

Young Henry gives him a searching glance as if trying to understand him and looking for signs of his willingness to change. "You must follow my instructions carefully," he says. "Freedom will come only when you find peace in your heart and share it with the others in this prison. After this comes the real test."

Henry is puzzled. "Peace? How does one find peace in a God-forsaken place like this? What riddle is this you speak of?"

"It's not a riddle. On the contrary, it is very simple. It's all about intention. If you intend to have peace, you'll find it."

In the past, Henry would have told him that there can only be peace when an authority rules over it. An authority strong enough to defend the laws that keep the peace. Peace is maintained when everyone honours this authority. He was taught this and did his best to fulfil this as king.

"That's still true," his son says as if he can read his mind. "However, not when man has corrupted the laws. Authority is to serve the well-being of all, not one's own lust for power or conquest. The law has to carry the intention of peace in one's heart, which can only be manifested with genuine compassion."

"Compassion?" Henry says sarcastically. "You sound like Desiderius Erasmus, whom I knew very well when I was young. He made false claims that war is not compatible with the Bible. Yet many great patriarchs went to war, such as Joshua, whose army brought Jericho to its knees. Then there was King David. His expansion of Israel absorbed the lands of the Philistines, Moab and others through wars of conquest. Did they apply compassion?"

Henry feels he has clarified his position, but his son does not seem willing to discuss the topic any further. "Alright, I'll aim for peace," Henry decides.

"And will you share this message with the other men here in prison?" His son presses.

"These men? They are all individualists. They cannot agree on anything."

"They'll listen," his son says, smiling mysteriously.

One of the prisoners yells out in pain. Henry looks away for a moment. He wants to ask his son why they will do so, but when he turns back, he discovers his son is no longer there.

Henry realises that what just occurred could change everything for him. He is willing to try and is moved to speak to the other prisoners through the iron bars of his cell.

"My fellow prisoners," Henry says loudly and confidently. "A miracle just took place here in these prison walls."

All the men stop talking and stare at him. "This man here," Henry says, pointing to the scholar with the beard, "was right all along. An important visitor came to see me just as he predicted. He was my firstborn son. His life on Earth was short-lived, but he has grown into a fine young man, a son that any father would be proud of. He told me we'll all be free."

The men are confused and suspicious. Some start hurling abuse at him.

"What conspiracy is this?" one of the prisoners yells.

"He's delusional. We never saw anyone here!" shouts another. "No one's coming to set us free. We are all destined for the pit."

"If you wonder how this could be," Henry says, "it's very simple. We must each initiate our freedom by praying for peace. When shared and lived as our highest moral principle, peace will set us free."

Some begin to wonder if this could be true and, out of desperation, begin to pray for peace, just as Henry did before his son's arrival. Young Henry's presence and energy have somehow ignited Henry and many of the prisoners with a renewed sense of faith.

He feels as if he has changed. He remembers how free he felt after listening to a piece of music or when he went out riding on his favourite stallion. It felt much the same as now— a euphoria, as if a heavy burden had been lifted.

"How do you know that the apparition was your son and not some evil spirit impersonating him?" the prisoner opposite him calls out from his dark cell. This catches Henry off guard, and he doesn't answer.

"We all should confess," the scholar says. "Let's share our stories and be witnesses to each other's confession. But keep your identity hidden. Who will go first?"

"He should start," Henry's neighbour points at him.

CHAPTER TWENTY-SIX
CONFESSIONS

HE CONTEMPLATES how he will start his confession, but before Henry can get around to it, one of the other prisoners volunteers to go first. He is relieved.

"I know why I'm here." A dirty, sickly-looking prisoner with a bloody gash to his head limps toward the gate in his cell. He is eager to tell his story. "I was an adventurer. Fearless, I travelled to many far-off places. Later in life, I involved myself in political matters and owned a large estate. I befriended His Majesty, who held me in high esteem, and I fought for him as a captain in his navy. My burden has made me a lonely and desperate soul searching for redemption. I'm forever haunted by the memory of that fateful day."

Henry looks at the man and tries to figure out who he is, but the darkness partially obscures his face, and Henry does not recognise his voice.

"The day before my death, I was made vice-admiral of the royal fleet and received a golden whistle from the king." The man's voice begins to crack. "The Mary Rose, his best warship, was entrusted to my care, along with a crew of about five hundred souls."

"George Carew…" Henry whispers. The poor wretch. Of all people to find him here. This is extraordinary.

Carew came as a young man to court, and Henry, who knew the young man's uncle well, had felt an instant affinity with the unruly, fun-loving young fellow. They became close friends. Years later, Henry decided he needed a trusted and determined man for

the battle in the Solent against the Gallic fleet along the straits
north of the Isle of Wight. Carew was made the new captain of
Henry's beloved *Mary Rose* the day before the battle.

"Never underestimate the French," Henry mutters while he
recalls the battle. It was the summer of 1545, and he had observed
the conflict from Southsea Castle.

"It wasn't the French who were the problem," Carew says.

Henry is surprised by his immediate response. Carew somehow
must have overheard him.

"When I was introduced to the members of my crew the day
before the battle, the second in command and the boatswain, I
found out they didn't want me there. Nobody paid me any respect.
I made an effort with the soldiers, the sailors, the gunners, the
surgeons, the trumpeters, the carpenter, the pilot, the cook and
even the barber-surgeon. I shook their hands and looked them in
the eye. It didn't make any difference. They all gave me the cold
shoulder as if I was the enemy."

Right from the start, the *Mary Rose* led the attack. This had
been Henry's battle plan all along.

"The king was confident the ship would prove to be a decisive
player and tip the balance in our favour," Carew adds. "After all,
she had won many previous battles. No one, including myself, ever
questioned his authority or ability to lead. He was a strong king,"
Carew says, and it sounds like he means it. This pleases Henry.

"When the enemy was in sight," Carew continues, "I gave the
orders, and she fired all the cannons from the starboard side. The
plan was to turn the ship and fire the cannons from the port side,
but while doing so, the ship leaned too far to the starboard side.
I yelled to everyone to move over to the port side, but it was too
late. The gun ports were wide open, the seawater flooded into the
ship's galley, and it capsized. There was no time to think or do
anything. Men were screaming and shouting in confusion. Some
jumped ship. The next thing I knew, an incredible force pulled us
all underwater. We didn't stand a chance."

Henry is moved to hear his friend's account.

"I was struck on the head by something heavy." Carew touches
the bloody gash on his head. "I don't remember any suffering or
pain after that or even how I drowned. Then the strangest thing

happened to me. I could see myself floating in the water from above, along with parts of the ship and all the men on it. I can still see the horror in their eyes. There were so many bodies floating in the water. It was awful. It felt like it was my mistake. I failed." Carew begins to weep with sorrow and regret.

The ship went down in a matter of minutes. Filled with a sense of doom, Henry had observed the tragedy. Later, he learned that only thirty members of the crew survived.

It is quiet in the prison. No one speaks. So many could have said something, and even Henry feels tempted to console Carew, but he doesn't. In his heart, he forgives his friend and absolves him of any blame. Sometimes silence can be more powerful than any words, and Henry can tell that all the men are affected by it.

"It's my turn!" Henry's neighbour opposite him shouts, stepping forward into the dim light of the dungeon. Henry is curious. The man stands up straight with a confidence that comes with maturity and importance.

"After hearing both of you speak, it's important that I convey to you that I, too, have left a trail of misery behind me. Nor do I wish to return to it. From now onwards, my only desire is to serve God and to invite you all to join me in a brotherhood of equals. Men before the Almighty. May we call upon the good forces available to us now in worship. Now, let us kneel and seek atonement."

The man kneels like a knight on one knee while his hands rest on the other. All the men in the dungeon except for Henry follow suit. Henry studies the man who sounds familiar to him.

"For me, the true spirit of the Reformation is God as a concept and an ideal of love and compassion that lives in all of us and should be celebrated by us as a brotherhood of equals." The prisoners react to his words by rising together.

Thomas Cromwell. How did Henry not recognise his first minister sooner? He does not look like he once did, far from it. He is emaciated and soiled with bruises all over his body. But the large droopy nose that defined Cromwell's face is the same as it always was.

"I wish we could have taken the Reformation a step further to create a society based on these principles," Cromwell says. "In this way, it would have been revolutionary. We would no longer think of hierarchies of power that create chaos but instead order in the form of democracy inspired by the principles of Spirit. From this, a peaceful society that could prosper and defend itself against the forces of evil would have been possible. My life didn't reflect these principles; that's why I'm here with you in Limbo. It was only toward the end of my life that I saw glimpses of what might be on the horizon, but the king stopped me."

The last remark insults Henry. "I'm confident the king knew better what to do than his first minister," he says.

"The king? He would throw frivolous tantrums and behave like a spoiled child when he didn't get his way. Although he did surprise me from time to time with a good idea." To hear his former minister ridicule him enrages Henry.

"Some write endless documents and think they are intelligent while others run a country," Henry replies, throwing Cromwell's remark back at him.

His neighbour stares at Henry. There is surprise in his eyes. Does he recognise him?

"Behind all the gold and the power, there's nothing to be proud of. His legacy will be that of the king who committed adultery and killed his wives. The irony is that he didn't even want to marry the woman—Anne Boleyn, that is. When they told him he couldn't marry her, the stubborn and obstinate man dug a hole he couldn't get out of and tried to convince himself it was all worth it. That's why I don't want to look back. There's only darkness and bitterness, evil and vanity. All of us have been weak, including me."

Henry is quiet. His true identity is known by the prisoners now.

"You treated Anne appallingly, but that's a cross you'll have to bear until you can find resolution," Cromwell says. There's blood on your hands. Seek repentance before it's too late. Join us."

The men shout at Henry to kneel before God, but Henry doesn't hear them. He is too busy pondering what Cromwell just said about Anne.

CHAPTER TWENTY-SEVEN
THE FUGITIVE

"HUSH. LET'S ALL BE QUIET," the scholar says in a raised voice. "We're all sinners here. Remember our friend's beautiful words about a brotherhood of equals inspired by the Spirit. It's not about the past anymore. It's about the future and how we can be free.

"I was a very old man when called to leave my life behind. I had been blind for several years before then. I wasn't bitter about it. The blindness brought me an inner peace that prepared me for the great departure. When it finally came during my sleep, I woke up with my eyesight restored."

"What brought you here?" Henry asks. "Who brought you here?"

"God did, to minister to those poor souls imprisoned by the suffering they have caused in the hope that they might seek repentance. As a man called to serve God, it is my duty." He looks directly at Henry. "You may remember me as your father's confessor."

Bishop Richard Foxe was a kind and educated man and the founder of Corpus Christi College, Oxford. Henry remembers he served his father from the early days in France, and guided and comforted him before his death. His father called him a "clever fox" who gave him prudent reasoning as to why everyone should pay the king's taxes like John Morton, Lord Chancellor, before him.

Foxe explained to the king that someone who lives the life of a wealthy man is clearly rich and can afford to pay a loving contribution, and those who live in a frugal and modest way must have been saving money, so they can afford to pay this benevolence as well. Shrewd, it certainly was.

"It's easier for a camel to go through the eye of a needle than for someone rich to enter the kingdom of heaven," Foxe says. There is regret in his voice. It has the sentiment of an apology, an acknowledgement of failure.

"As Jesus said: 'Sell all that you own and distribute the money to the poor, and you'll have treasure in heaven.'" The scholar sighs. "For the love of money is the root of all evil. Like many in a powerful position, I forgot my responsibilities and orchestrated a plan to take from the poor."

Henry is quiet. He knows all of this, of course, and reflects on his own sins. There are many, and now the bishop is here with him as he had been with his father in his last days. He ponders if this is by design. Should he confess his sins to the bishop here? Before these men who had once served him?

"I didn't experience any of this," one of the prisoners not far from Henry states in a broad, deep voice. "All I remember when the time came was a constant knocking on the wall. When I asked those attending me what was happening, they didn't understand what I was talking about. They told me that they couldn't hear a thing."

"What happened next?" someone asks.

"Well, everything changed, of course."

"What do you mean?"

"I guess I died."

"What did you see? Where were you?"

"Ah, yes, that was interesting. I was in a French garden that looked very pretty and manicured, as these gardens do. I figured I must be in the Loire Valley at one of King Francis's castles. A little boy was playing, and I thought that maybe he was the king's son, but then at the far end of the garden, I saw Mary, my wife, who I lost far too early in life. She appeared with our two little boys." The man stops there. The memory makes him tearful.

Henry notices it and stares with disbelief. "Who are you?" he asks impatiently. He needs to know. There is a lot of emotion in his voice.

"No names, please!" the scholar shouts from the other side of the dungeon. The man looks Henry straight in the eye.

"Tell me," Henry urges.

"Names have no importance here," his neighbour says. "Talking with all of you makes me realise we're all friends. Family. We are all we've got."

"Oh, shut up, man," Henry says, perturbed. Could it be him? Charles Brandon? His longtime friend who grew up at his father's court and later married his sister, Mary?

"If you are who I think you are, you're family indeed, and not only that. You've also lost a considerable amount of weight, my friend," Henry says, chuckling.

"Not as much as you," Brandon replies, and they both laugh. Charles's reply makes Henry aware he is not the only one who has figured out the identity of the others. Why would they not just all come out and say it?

It turns out that when he looks around the dungeon, there are moments he becomes aware of the men's previous identities and connections in life.

Richard Long and Walter Walsh, wealthy courtiers and members of Henry's privy chamber, are also among the men.

Henry counts how many of them there are. Including himself, there are twelve. That is a good number. The amazing thing is that all of them are his friends and previous members of his privy chamber.

"I have a feeling I know all of you," Henry says. "Even though we may look different and are not the same person we once were."

"That's true," Foxe agrees. "We still carry the shadow of our previous lives, yet on the wall here, we see a glimpse of the light of our future."

"Are these not the flames of the eternal hellish fire we imagined?" Carew asks.

"No," Foxe insists.

"How do you know?" Carew asks.

"One just knows," Henry says. "It's like when you talk to your horse. You don't need words or a language to speak to each other. You just know. You share your thoughts and become one. I've experienced that on many occasions."

"That's so true," Brandon agrees. "Words aren't required. It's a great feeling when it's like that. Mary and I shared that connection."

"Just like us here now," Foxe confirms. The men bond together as their old friendships are reignited.

Henry, who holds the iron gate with both hands, leans forward to get a better view of the men. Suddenly, the gate squeaks open.

"By Jove," Henry mutters, then steps out into the hallway of the dungeon. Astonished, the others look at him.

Carew pushes against the gate of his cell. It opens as well. Foxe and all the others follow suit.

"We're free," Foxe says. There is a moment of disbelief in Foxe and all of them, but not for long.

"Let's find out where we are," Foxe says, then starts walking toward the corner of the hallway.

Around the corner from their cells, at the end of a long hallway, the men discover an opening that leads into a large, ruined cathedral. The twelve men walk into its nave. As they do, their appearance changes. They are no longer battered and bruised but young and full of vigour. Their clothing is pristine, too, of the kind men of nobility would wear.

An altar dedicated to the Virgin Mary with many candles stands in the middle. It is the glow from the candles that reflects on the wall the men were looking at from their cells. Henry was right after all.

Curious, all the men look around. The cathedral roof has fallen in, and most of the stained glass windows are broken. Glass, rubble, and dust are strewn across the hard stone floor.

"Look! These are the ruins of seven cathedrals in total," Foxe says. "They once stood on a hill. In the centre of it is this holy chapel, or what's left of it."

"How do you know that?" Carew asks, but Foxe does not need to answer. All the men can see in their minds the drawings with the fine details of the amazing architecture of the seven cathedrals. And while they see it in their minds, the walls and stained glass windows repair themselves, and the vault above them returns. Everything that was damaged is restored and made new in such a way it takes their breath away.

Some of the men fall on their knees in front of the altar with its wall of wooden sculptures and a larger-than-life statue of the Madonna, while others look around the cathedral, bewildered and repentant. They are no longer alone either.

Many men and women, all dressed in simple white robes, have come from nowhere and have filled up the nave, the chancel and the choir loft. Some of them are recognisable as loved ones.

It is difficult to stay together as a group of twelve, and Henry is cut off from the others, finding himself alone. At first, he wants to call them back and ask them to wait for him, but the other men are caught up in the crowd of their loved ones. He decides to get some air and finds a quiet corner in the cathedral.

He studies the architecture of the building and looks up at the crowning part at the top of one of the columns nearby. It shows sculpted demons. It is an innocent image, but he wonders why it is there. It intrigues him, and the longer he looks at it, the more real the little demons seem. Just when he becomes aware that one of their faces seems alive and has a devilish smirk, he hears hooves.

Henry turns around. Behind him, in the large cathedral doorway, stands Canicida. The handsome stallion makes a light nicker and raises his head, looking at Henry. Henry smiles and gently strokes the horse.

"You're happy to see me, aren't you?"

Canicida snorts. The stallion looks so tall and conspicuous.

"What a beautiful horse you are," Henry whispers, looking at him with admiration.

"My most loyal and faithful friend."

The cathedral doorway leads to a sunny field beyond, with glowing mountains as a backdrop in the distance. Henry had not seen this before, but when Canicida whinnies again, he does not hesitate and mounts the horse.

"Good horse," Henry whispers, moving the horse around to face the open gate. Step by step, Canicida walks toward the gate. Just before Henry is about to pass through the gate, he looks over his shoulder at the crowd behind him in the restored cathedral.

In the nave, right in the middle of the crowd, he spots his good friend, Charles Brandon, Duke of Suffolk. He still looks as inconspicuous as all the others who were in the prison, and it touches Henry to see his good friend there. He raises his hand and smiles. Brandon notices him and bows briefly.

Next to Brandon stands his wife, Mary Tudor, Henry's sister and the former Queen of France. Their union was a true love affair, and they married secretly without telling Henry, which was an act of treason at the time, but Henry forgave them, of course. What else could he have done?

Mary notices Henry as well and nods at him. For a moment, Henry hesitates. Should he go back and greet them?

"Now, go!" Henry yells instead, spurring Canicida into a gallop, and they ride out into the fields beyond.

CHAPTER TWENTY-EIGHT
A GATHERING

ANNE'S MANOR HOUSE, her hideaway, is covered with dust, and many windows are cracked. It does not matter to her, and she ignores it. Instead, she focuses on the model of Utopia on display. It has been completed, and she positions a chair next to it.

Despite all the destruction around her, she is curious about this new world she is creating. She has not seen the latest additions yet, so she explores the finer details of the current design.

It strikes her not only how precise it is but also how real it seems with the water in the river, the palm trees, the statues and the pillars of the temples, and the hanging gardens with their flowers in full bloom and ripe fruits. Even the people, she discovers, look real. They seem to move around from one place to another, although she thinks it is probably her imagination.

She brings her face closer to the model of the city and looks at a female figure on one of the broad marble steps leading to the river. The woman is wearing a white robe with borders of gold and has her hair rolled up in an ancient Greek fashion. She is in her late twenties. She looks up to Anne. It is so strange that it makes Anne giggle. The woman waves at her. Anne chuckles. This is better than telling herself a story.

Anne waves back. The woman gestures for Anne to follow her. Where is she going?

At the top of the steps, an enormous rectangular gate rises. The woman hurries through it and comes out at the other side, where there are more steep steps to climb, leading to an even larger building with high walls covered with immense frescos displaying all kinds of figures, animals and shapes in many lively colours.

Another gate stands tall in front of her. Many steps come together here, and many more are ahead of her. Anne feels so connected to the young woman in Utopia that it feels like she is there herself. Through the woman's eyes, she looks up at the towering walls of what looks like a temple. How far do these steps go? What a beautiful city.

The buildings seem to rise into the sky. There is so much to discover here. And everyone seems so friendly. They all smile at her. Children surround her and playfully rush up and down the steps. They all seem happy. A soft breeze touches her skin together with the warm rays of the sun.

"Mama! Mama!" A little girl shouts. A baby's cry follows the shouts.

Shocked, Anne sits straight up. Completely alert. She gets up from her chair and hurries toward Elizabeth's room. Did the crying come from there?

The room is empty, as always. Nothing has changed. She sighs deeply. She must have imagined it, but why did she hear the crying?

She picks up one of the dolls and holds it against her chest. "It will all be okay," she whispers and lulls the doll as if it is Elizabeth. She takes the doll with her and holds it tightly as she walks through the house. She finally lies down on the bed.

"You can lie on the pillow next to me," she says to the doll, then rearranges one of the pillows and gently lays the doll on top. This is exactly what she did with Elizabeth when she was a baby.

Sentimental, maybe, as most mothers from her class in society would not do such a thing, instead handing over the responsibility to a servant. Anne, however, ignored the protocols. She enjoyed spending time with her baby and seeing her up close, next to her. It made her happy.

"You're safe with me," she says, smiling.

When Anne falls asleep, she dreams of walking through a long, narrow tunnel. She almost suffocates, as if there is no air. In a hurry, she reaches out to a door and, with lots of effort, can open it, despite strong resistance from the other side. When it finally swings open, the enormous force of a strong wind coming out of the darkness of the night throws her against the wall.

Who or what is out there? Anne feels the presence of someone lurking in the darkness not far from her. It is a man, and he is extremely angry and violent. She wants to run away and tries to lift her arms to defend herself, but her entire body feels paralysed. Her heart is racing, and she is breathing fast. "Help me, please!" she screams.

When she wakes up, she still feels the man's presence in the room with her. She pulls the blankets up to her chin. He is out there, and she waits for his next move with trepidation. Nothing happens. She waits until the door to her bed chamber creaks open. A woman enters, the same woman she saw inside the model of Utopia. She appears as a ghostly figure surrounded by light.

"Anne," she says with a soothing, gentle voice. Her presence lights up the room. "Come with me." The smile on her face is warm and caring.

Anne wants to, but she shakes her head. She is afraid. Not now. She cannot go. Not without Elizabeth.

When her lady-in-waiting appears the next morning and walks around oblivious to the chaos around her, Anne does not talk about her nightmare. Instead, she tells her that she realised something very important during the night.

"Did you know I never received a proper funeral? I think that's a great injustice," Anne says while she sits up straight in bed with her clothes on. "I must mourn my own death and those who died with me. I've decided that the entire house should be draped in black— all the walls, windows, and furniture. Herbs should be found, especially rosemary sprigs that can be pinned to the sleeves of my gowns. Mourning rings with the image of a skeleton or cross should be made available, and all those attending me should wear black gloves." Anne explains.

Anne is less sure about other things. "The tolling of bells is unnecessary," she thinks aloud, "but everyone and everything should be as during a real funeral. Some ale, wine and spirits should be put out for those attending in spirit."

"Who are the others, milady, that you want to pay respect to?" the lady-in-waiting asks.

"My dearest brother George, of course, and Henry Norris, Mark Smeaton, Francis Weston and William Brereton," she says. She is pleased with this until she remembers something else. "But it's not only their deaths; it also marks my separation from Elizabeth. I want to mourn the mother I wasn't allowed to be."

The lady-in-waiting nods and readies herself to leave the room and begin the preparations.

"Do you think I should lie in bed as if I am lying in state?" Anne asks. This is a dilemma because if she lies in bed and is dead, how can she tell if everything will be done properly?

The lady-in-waiting thinks about it for a moment. "You shouldn't lie in bed. I think you should be yourself and receive your guests." Anne nods in agreement. Yes, that seems to be the best way forward.

"But who will come?" the lady-in-waiting asks. "Who are the guests?"

This is a good question, but Anne knows precisely how she wants it. "There won't be any real guests. I don't want to see anyone. They must be actors; all they should do is mourn with me. Fulfil the ritual. I want to feel it's a proper funeral, but I don't want to talk to anyone."

"Of course, milady. I'll organise it exactly as you want it to be; you can be assured of that."

"I'll need a special gown and your help getting dressed. Something simple, respectful, yet demure," Anne adds.

"Yes, of course," the lady-in-waiting says, then rushes away.

And so it happens. The entire palace is draped in black, and Anne gets dressed in a black gown, mantle and matching black hood draped with lace.

"It will be too warm," she tells the lady-in-waiting but decides to wear it for an hour or so. She looks as if she has come from outside as she visits her own deathbed. She also puts on a mourning ring decorated with a skull, and a rosemary sprig is pinned to her sleeve.

The rooms are filled with candles and are completely transformed. A handful of guests has already arrived.

Among them is a man of the faith who prays out loud. Against Anne's instructions, someone starts to toll the bells. The lady-in-waiting approaches Anne nervously to tell her that it was a misunderstanding, but Anne reassures her and tells her it creates the appropriate atmosphere and that it will be suitable for an hour or so.

Satisfied, Anne observes the gathering of mourners. While she does, she thinks back to the men who died with her and contemplates the indescribable ruin the king brought upon all of their families.

CHAPTER TWENTY-NINE
ALONE WITH NATURE

CANICIDA GALLOPS through the open fields and over the rolling hills in front of them. At first, Henry debated if he should return to the cathedral to embrace his sister, but something beckoned him not to.

Also, his desire to be free and outside in the open air was too strong, and even though he was fond of his sister and found her good company, he understood her presence in the cathedral was to be there for Brandon. She did not come for him.

No one came to see him. It is what it is, and to be back in what looks like the English countryside on a sunny day is a marvellous alternative to a family reunion.

Henry leans forward and prompts Canicida to gallop even faster. "At least I found you waiting for me," he says.

Later, they take a break near a stream. Henry finds a spot in the green grass to sit down and reflect while Canicida bends his head to drink some cool, refreshing water.

The chirping of a swallow makes Henry look up. It is perched in one of the trees nearby, but it quickly flies away into the afternoon sun. He is amused by it. It reminds him of Anne.

She loves nature, or she once did. It gave her the feeling of freedom. Its beauty was proof to her that God's creation was fundamentally good. It was mankind that corrupted it with greed, war and pestilence. She would often share profound thoughts like this with him, which was one of the things he loved about her.

He lies back in the grass and allows his thoughts of her to rise to the surface. He remembers her love of flowers. Every spring, when the flower was in bloom, she would fill her quarters with the delicate, sweet scent of lily of the valley.

Yellow was Anne's favourite colour, which she said gave her hope and joy. She often chose to wear it, but he suspected that she liked it for no other reason than to draw attention to herself, and indeed, it always worked. Men flocked to her like moths to a burning candle, unaware of the danger awaiting them. He was one of those men. Her charisma was irresistible.

He reflects on why her hold on him was so powerful and finally begins to understand it. It was not merely because he wanted a son and was looking for an alternative wife, as some suggested.

As a king, he was never alone, not even when he was in bed or asleep. He was always attended, servants waiting in the wings to provide anything he desired.

Despite all this, he felt deeply alone. Yes, there were his friends, the entertainment, the sports, the hunts and the many festivities they all shared, but deep down, he carried a burden of failure. The camaraderie of his male friends and the warmth and laughter that came with it was not enough to take the weight away.

It was more existential than that. It was a desire to feel fully alive and triumph despite life's limitations. And for a man who loved women, only a woman could offer him that, and for him, sadly, that woman was no longer Catherine but Anne. She lifted his spirits and made him feel alive and fulfilled.

Did he treat her wrongly? The tragic truth, or so he believed at the time, was that Anne threatened him and the throne. She was too ambitious and stubborn to accept her place, as Catherine had done before her. Besides that, Anne and Norris were far too amicable with each other. Cromwell was right about that.

Most importantly, Henry knew in his heart that God did not favour his second marriage. Anne had tricked him into it. He gets angry now. Why did nobody understand he had to do what he had to do? As the king. For England.

"The hour of one's death is the time for truth, reflection and repentance," Anne had said sarcastically. She had said many other things, mostly unpleasant and false accusations.

Once there was genuine love between them. Even Catherine had recognised that. Everyone did. Annoyed, he asks himself why Anne is suddenly at the forefront of his mind. For him, the story is simple. He can twist it around and over analyse it, but that fact does not disappear. It depresses him now to think of her.

As if on command, the blue sky darkens. Henry gets up and mounts his horse.

"Come on, Canicida, we're leaving." He feels impatient and has lost his good mood. Canicida has found some clovers and is enjoying himself. "You clever boy," Henry says.

He looks at the sky. A sombre formation of clouds blocks out the sun.

"Woah," he says with a firm and commanding voice, bringing Canicida to a halt. Moments ago, the place looked idyllic. Now there is a darkness to it.

"Travel with peace in your heart" is Young Henry's motto. Henry has a soft spot for the lad, but the duke never lived and so never had to deal with the brutality and disappointments of being human. His son would have discovered that those who are aggressive in society are the ones who climb the ladder and achieve their goals.

Henry saw it happen again and again. Those with an insatiable appetite, the competitive and unscrupulous ones, succeed. What would have become of the country if he had put his faith in the good of mankind? Henry is a realist. He would not have lasted long as a king and would not have become the successful monarch he was if he hadn't followed the path chosen.

"We're going to check out that building over there," he says to Canicida while he looks at a large manor that has come into view. The horse whinnies and begins cantering toward it.

CHAPTER THIRTY
HENRY'S ARRIVAL

HENRY'S HEART RACES as he rides closer to the manor house. He cannot explain why, but it feels like something important will happen there, something that will help change the course of his journey. A reunion, perhaps, or a new beginning. Whatever it is, the force drawing him there is too powerful to resist.

The building itself does not support his suspicion. Everything indicates it is deserted. No smoke is coming from the chimneys, and the entire construction with its red-orange bricks is in disrepair. Some of the windows are broken, while many are covered up.

Surrounding the property are large gardens. They look unkempt, and most of the bushes and trees are stripped bare of their leaves and flowers. The strange thing is the gardens are not overgrown with weeds.

Canicida and Henry are in front of a wooden bridge. The pond under it is connected to a stream, but there is hardly any water in it. What a stark contrast with the lush green hills he travelled through earlier. What has happened here?

Henry takes a closer look at the black mud in the ditch below. There are traces of dead fish and birds. Whatever did this left a devastating mark.

"Come on, boy," he says to Canicida, who baulks at crossing the bridge. After the bridge, they pass through a gate. Then Canicida gallops over a path through the lifeless gardens toward a red-brick hall. A heavy oak door, banded with iron, is at the front with moulded terracotta *amorini* above it. Their presence provides a warm welcome to the house. Henry dismounts his horse and decides to go inside and explore.

The manor is deserted, as he suspected, and the main hall is empty and dark. The windows have oiled linen in front of them and wooden shutters, which he finds odd and old-fashioned. In itself, it is a safe and warm place to live, he concludes when he checks out the fireplaces, but where is all the furniture? Who owns it?

He walks through the long hallways, only to find more empty rooms, until he enters a large hall with tall windows. Some of the windows are draped in black. A large model city is displayed on a table in the centre.

To find a scale model of this size in this deserted place is very odd. It is a fascinating model of what looks like a city from the ancient world, with its white buildings, architecture, columns and sculptures. But why is it here? The model's gardens and the water running through the aqueducts draw his attention. It is all very real.

A noise in the background startles him. He looks around. Is anyone there? It is quiet again, but he gets the feeling someone is there. He walks over to a door leading to the next room.

There. Again he hears something. Someone must be there. Slowly, he opens the door. The room is small, and there are candles burning in front of an altar.

It looks like a chapel. A large painting with a toddler hangs on the wall.

"Elizabeth…" Shocked, he stares at it. It hits him hard. In this faraway, hostile world, seeing her lovely face deeply affects him. Curious, he walks over to it. Elizabeth looks so real in the painting. It is a very accurate portrayal of her as a little girl. It makes him realise how much he loves her and misses her.

With disbelief, he sees the christening dress and toys. He picks them up. These are exact replicas. He recognises them and lovingly touches them.

"I pray for her daily," a woman says.

"Anne?" he exclaims, turning around.

She is standing in the doorway behind him. Her face is drained of colour, her hollow cheeks sickly, and her hair unruly. She is still dressed in black as though in mourning.

"You look awful," he says. It is true; she does. She has not taken care of herself. Her eyes look wild and suspicious, like a mad woman tormented by ghosts and delusions.

"There's nothing you can say or do that will affect me," she says angrily. "You're of no importance anymore. I'm free of you now."

He does not dignify her remark with an answer. Instead, he looks around the room. It is like a chapel, but there is dust, chips of plaster and pieces of glass everywhere. What on earth is going on with her?

"Why have you come?" she asks.

Not knowing how to answer her, Henry shuffles back and forth, puts the dress back, and looks at the painting again.

"It's a lovely portrait," he says. "I didn't know it was made at the time."

"It's an image from my memory," she says. "My imagination created it. Memories are all I have left of our daughter."

"Is that so?"

"At first, I feared I would forget how she looks and smells or how her voice sounds. It's astonishing, but I remember everything—every detail of her. The painting helps, but I don't need it. It's all in here." She lays her hand on her heart. "Not to be with her and not to know how she is has been the worst part of my passing," she says, her face sad. "There's no greater punishment than that. It's been a tremendous struggle to keep myself going."

She gives him a long look as if she expects an answer. For a moment, he wonders if he should tell her about Elizabeth. Does she want to know? And does she want to hear it from him?

"She's fine," he says.

His statement shocks her. There is a sudden anguish in her eyes that was not there before, a rawness. It unsettles him.

"She really is," he insists. "Elizabeth and I quarrelled quite a bit, actually." He chuckles. "She's just like me. In everything, really."

Anne does not acknowledge it. Her eyes have turned cold and reveal emotions he never saw in her before, as if she could explode with fury any moment. He decides to ignore it. What else can he do?

"She's so much unlike the other two," he says.

Anne looks up but is silent.

"Mary and Edward," he adds. It occurs to him that she does not know about Edward even though he thought he mentioned him before.

Anne merely nods without asking any further questions. He decides to explain the matter further. "She's third in line to the throne through an Act of Succession. It's all properly set out in this way."

With anguish, she looks at him and wrings her hands. It is strange the way she behaves. She clears her throat as if she is about to say something but does not.

"What?" he asks her.

She turns her face away from him and looks at the floor. "I wondered if she ever asked about me," she says. Anne looks broken and vulnerable. Henry's instinct is to answer her immediately, but he stops himself. Elizabeth never asked or spoke about her mother, and she was wise not to.

Anne turns to him again. "I have to know," she says with fearful eyes.

"No. Not to me," he replies. He does not want to lie to her. There is no outburst of anger. Anne simply nods and seems to reflect on it.

"Does she get along with the others? Do they like her?"

He is taken aback by the questions. He realises he probably should not be surprised by them. She misses Elizabeth. As a result, he does not respond in his usual impulsive and impatient manner. Instead, he tries to be considerate.

"They all like her. Especially Edward. They're very close, as a matter of fact. Elizabeth helps him with his learning. She is very intelligent. She's a lot of fun too. In many ways, she is like you."

Anne is touched hearing him speak about their daughter with warmth. This may seem odd or curious to Anne, but that is how it is. He and Elizabeth were close.

"That's good," she says softly.

He looks through the doorway to her drawing room. He is struck by the black drapes and the funeral atmosphere in the room. "Is this where you live?" he asks. Apart from the sombre atmosphere, the room reminds him of Hever Castle, where Anne grew up. It is mostly the scale and the intimacy of the room. He stayed at the castle several times himself. The Boleyns were always very welcoming to him.

When he looks at Anne in these sorrowful surroundings, he feels pity for her. It is not a feeling of empathy or warmth but merely an observation of her demise.

As he stands there looking at her, he suddenly wonders why he is there. What brought him there?

CHAPTER THIRTY-ONE
THE PERFECT STORM

O F COURSE, she can tell him to go away. She wonders if, in these new realms, she has that power over him. Can she ask her servant to throw him out? She decides not to test it. Not yet, at least.

He does not intimidate her. Instead, he looks out of sorts, like a lost soul. He is a shadow of the man or the king he once was. Even his voice, which was always strong, melodic, and very distinct, sounds subdued and lacks confidence. His once booming voice is now the voice of someone weak and in distress. She still can read him, though, as she could when they were alive.

While she has these thoughts, it suddenly dawns on her. If she ignores him, he will disappear again. That is how it works around here. It is as easy as that, and for a moment, she feels he fades away into nothingness like a shadow usurped by the darkness. It is a peculiar moment in which she must decide whether to allow him to vanish or to invite him to stay around a little longer. Does she want him to disappear?

"You don't seem to be sure," he says.

She looks at him, astonished. "Not sure about what?"

He smirks. "If you want to engage with me or not."

"That's right. I'm not sure." She waits for a moment and stands with her back toward him.

"I feel sorry for you," he says.

Anne turns toward him, disbelief on her face. Like a mad woman, she starts to laugh. This unsettles him, she can tell, but she doesn't care. It makes her laugh even louder.

"What's wrong with you? Have you gone mad?" There is frustration in his voice and eyes, but he regrets what he just said. Anne stops laughing.

"It's funny," she says, "that you pity me." She starts laughing again. It upsets him even more.

"You better stop," he warns her.

She steps toward him, her eyes wild with rage. "What else can you do to me?" she asks as if she is trying to provoke him.

"You're behaving foolishly," he replies, clearly feeling uncomfortable.

"I want you to go," she says, but she realises the moment to make that happen has passed. She is now upset about her indulgence with him.

"If that's what you want," he says. Of course, they both know that he will stay and that they will have a conversation.

Anne walks away from him, disappears into the drawing room, and then sits on one of the stools with an ornamented back. Henry follows her but waits in the doorway. He takes in the shabby atmosphere of the drawing room and everything inside it.

She ignores him and stares at the rug on the tiles in front of her. "It's worn out," she says. "How can that be?"

Henry steps into the room and walks over to the fireplace which has been lit.

"It's threadbare and tattered," she says. Henry is silent. She stares into the room and reflects on it. "Hardly anyone ever comes here, so why would it be like this?"

Anne's train of thought is interrupted by a loud hammering sound at one of the windows. Half of the window is covered on the outside with a wooden panel that is being nailed to the window. They both stare at it in alarm.

Her lady-in-waiting appears. "What's going on outside?" Anne asks her.

The woman's head drops, and she doesn't reply right away.

"Tell me," Anne presses.

"They are putting wooden panels in front of all the windows," the lady-in-waiting says, distressed. "There is a mighty storm coming."

"In front of all the windows?" Anne is surprised to hear this.

"Yes, milady, and in front of the doors as well," the woman says. "Very soon, no one will be able to leave. Not until the storm has passed."

"A storm…" Anne reflects on the apparition of the horsemen she saw in the sky. The memory sends a chill through her, but she does not tell Henry about it. Instead, she looks at him with pity. They are no doubt coming for him—or maybe for them both. She hadn't thought of that before. The locusts that destroyed her beautiful gardens were proof of their power.

"I'll bring out more candles," the lady-in-waiting says. "I hope the storm does not last very long." She takes her leave to begin her preparations.

Anne is left alone again with Henry. The room carries an awkward silence. She is rather anxious and shocked at the thought of the two of them spending any length of time together.

"I'm sure she's exaggerating," Henry says to reassure them both.

She finds his behaviour strange. It is out of character for him not to take charge and order everyone around. He does not raise his voice or even show impatience. Maybe he has changed?

Outside, the pounding of the wind and rain intensifies. A second and third panel, and even a fourth, are hammered in place, and the drawing room falls into darkness except for the light of the fireplace.

"You can still leave," Anne says, a slight panic in her voice. "I'm sure the door is still open. It must be."

The lady-in-waiting returns with a candelabra with four candles. She is dressed as though ready to depart. A long, black, hooded cape covers her gown.

"You can put it on the bureau," Anne says. The light of the candles throws long shadows and gives their faces a ghostly appearance.

"Madam," the woman says. "They told me I am to leave this house. The house may not survive the storm. Please come with me, madam."

"Really?" Anne gives it some thought. "I'll stay here," she says upon reflection, then looks at Henry. He ignores the woman's words and sits on the chair next to Anne's writing bureau.

"I would like to leave now," the woman says anxiously.

"Who will serve me when you're gone?" Anne asks the woman, who has a guilty look on her face. She does not know how to respond to this.

"Of course, you need to go," Anne says. "And thank you for assisting me. I'll manage without you, but you should leave before it's too late."

The woman does not have to think long. She does a quick curtsy and then rushes out the door, closing it behind her.

CHAPTER THIRTY-TWO
ANNE'S FURY

THEY SIT ALONE in the drawing room.

"We'll be safe," he tells her as if it matters what he thinks. Anne looks up at him without acknowledging his remark. As they sit together in silence, the only sound is the wind howling around the manor. Anne tries to ignore it.

"It's strange," she says. "I just remembered a dream I had long ago."

Henry looks up at her. "What was it about?"

"A man was standing alongside a road somewhere in the countryside. I couldn't see his face, as he had hidden it in the darkness of his cloak, but I knew he was a lonesome, down-and-out traveller, someone who had turned away from God and committed many wrongs in his life.

"I was curious to know who he was, so I followed him, and while I observed him, I noticed how he talked to the trees in the forest and how he listened to the rustling of the leaves. Later when it turned dark, the man looked up at the stars. He admired what he saw and thought God's glory was magnificent. It was at that moment that, by the gift of grace, he knew he was forgiven.

"Whilst observing him, I concluded he lacked faith in the unconditional gift he had received and rejected it. As a punishment, he was destined to be alone. Then from nowhere, a flock of birds arrived and started to circle him. They were hostile toward him and began to attack him. It became so bad he had to flee from them."

She tells Henry how she pitied the man, as she knew he was very much an outcast and not welcomed by others, and decided to stay with him in the dream.

"Not much later, he approached a fire," she says. "It was in a riverbed not far from a pond. Another man was sitting beside the fire. My lonesome traveller joined the stranger who welcomed him. At that moment, the traveller realised it was good not to be alone but to be in someone else's company. When he looked at the pond, he discovered that a large fish, almost as big as the pond itself, was swimming in it. The man was pleased by the presence of the fish and saw it as a sign of spiritual fulfilment. When he looked up at the sky, he was surprised and in awe. Towering above him was Jesus Himself. Our Lord looked down on him and blessed the man with redemption. He was made whole and renewed."

"I can't make sense of it," Henry says after a while, puzzled. "When did you have this dream? Were you with me at the time? It sounds like the dream might have been about me. What do you think?"

Anne looks at Henry, confusion in her eyes, as if she doubts him and pities him. "Maybe," she says. He looks so weary now, even fragile. She smiles faintly.

"I think it is. You always understood me well," Henry says, looking at Anne for reassurance. "What?" he asks her. "Don't you agree?"

"I think the man in the dream could've been anybody. I heard someone say that every character in a dream is part of the dreamer. In that way, I think the lonesome traveller was me," Anne says. "Maybe we're all like that sometimes. Isolated and disconnected, unwilling to trust in love but only to discover it's better to be with someone."

"Do you really think that?" he asks. Henry seems to like what she just said. She nods in agreement and seems comfortable being with him. Together they sit in silence and listen to the storm outside and the crackling fire.

"Anne, I've been thinking about the things you said, and I'm sorry if I wronged you." Surprised, she listens as he continues to speak. "I deeply regret my actions. My jealousy and pride got the better of me."

Anne stares at the fire and listens to her hurried breathing. "When I saw you again after your death," she says finally, "I was excited, sad, angry and exasperated all at once. And when I addressed the court, I felt strong and pleased that I could do this in such a collected and calm way. I felt vindicated."

"You had the mob supporting you," Henry replies.

"The mob?" She laughs in disbelief. "That was nothing compared to what happened to me when I was alive, and you were in control of it all." Her voice is harsh now, her eyes cold and bitter.

"Where were you when the verdict was reached? All the queens were there except you."

He is talking about the Court of Heaven with Catherine of Aragon, Jane Seymour and Catherine Howard.

She looks at him and pities him. Then a wave of anger rises in her. "At first, I wanted to join it and thought it could be beautiful and powerful to share this with the other women. I even prepared a speech. I decided that if I went, I would tell them that, on reflection, I can honestly say you raped me."

Her choice of words baffles and shocks him. He thinks she has spent too much time alone and must have turned mad.

"You raped me psychologically, emotionally and spiritually. You took everything I had, and then you wanted more, and when you discovered I had no more to give, you disregarded me as you do with food that has gone bad and lost its flavour." She pauses for a moment. "You forced your love and lust on me, as you did with my sister, Mary, before me. You used us as you used all the other women in your life."

Henry looks angry now. Something of his old self comes back alive. "This is a lie. I never pursued your sister. It was Mary who offered herself to me. It's true, and may I add, she did so willingly."

All her calmness is gone. He has wounded her again, and will do so repeatedly. Her face is white, like a ghost in the light of the tapers. She looks him in the eye. "You're a monster," she whispers.

Henry smirks and shrugs. She clenches her hands and shakes her head in disbelief. "You took me away from Elizabeth and denied her my love." There are no tears, and her face does not show the grief she has lived with for so long now. She looks livid.

"I hope she will be a better person than I ever could be. I pray she will believe in herself and be a force for good. I pray that she'll never be dependent on any man. I hope that men and women will be equal one day and that she will have the freedom to choose who and whatever she wants to be."

Henry stands up and starts pacing. He is uncomfortable. She ignores him at first, but after a while, he annoys her.

"Please stop pacing, she says. "If you have something to say, say it."

Henry stops pacing and looks at her in a strange way, as if he has never seen her before.

"You were special," he says. "So, there you have it. You were delightful. It's true. No other woman could compare to you. Forget everything I ever said before. Especially about Jane or your sister, Mary."

Anne does not know what to make of it. Finally, she shrugs. "It doesn't matter."

"But it does," Henry says. "Our love could've been the greatest love affair of all time."

Baffled, all she can do is shake her head. "Even now, it's all about you and what you feel."

A muted, faraway thunder followed by the gentle pitter-patter of rain comes from outside. They both listen to it.

"I can tell you're still angry with me," Henry says after a while. "All I know is that you wanted me as badly as I wanted you. There was a fire between us, an electrical charge. Something shameless and passionate but also joyful and breath-taking."

The storm outside intensifies and starts to sound like a torrent of rain. Without an explanation, she stands up.

"What's wrong?" Henry asks.

"I want to see if everything is alright in the chapel."

"Do you want me to join you?"

She does not know what to say, so she starts to walk away.

"Anne?" Henry says when she is about to leave the room. She stops and turns to him.

"What do you want from me?" she asks, a harsh tone in her voice. "Do you want me to scream and shout at you? Do you want me to throw myself on the floor and crawl like a wounded animal?

Do you want me to get a knife and stab it into my gut and rip myself open? What do you want?"

Bewildered at first, Henry looks at her.

"I was wrong," he says. "I've been wrong in many ways." There is a glimpse of despair in his eyes that she has never seen before.

"Can you forgive me?"

She tries to figure out what she feels about all of this, but her mind goes blank.

The hallway is dark, and she hesitates, wondering if she should return and fetch a candelabra, but she is relieved to be away from him. She does not want to see him anymore. His presence has disrupted her peace and her balance. He always had this effect on her.

He always wanted things to go his way. That was one reason why she refused him in those early days. She found him overwhelming.

The storm that is raging outside reflects how she feels about him. It makes the whole building shake. For a moment, she stands still and listens to it.

In the chapel, she finds Elizabeth's altar is still there. Her image and large portrait are intact and surrounded by roses and candles. Anne kneels in front of the altar. "Please, God, help lift this burden from me." As she prays, tears roll down her cheeks.

CHAPTER THIRTY-THREE
LOVE LETTERS

HENRY IS ALONE in the drawing room. The panels and tapestries that hang inside the room shake and quiver with every clap of thunder. Water drips from the ceiling onto the floor, and parts of the walls with no coverings have water running down them.

He is not afraid. The storm will pass. It is Anne and her accusations that are on his mind. He wants to make peace with her, but she does not seem to want that. Maybe he should make a grand gesture when she returns and ask again for forgiveness. From where he stands, Anne looks weak and does not resemble the striking woman she once was. He finds it interesting that on one person's face he can see beauty and ugliness simultaneously. He could always see that in her. For him, it made her different from all the others.

She was not as pleasing as her sister, but she could be mesmerising and charismatic, even though there were moments when he found her unattractive and off-putting. What was it about her that could provoke such a wide range of deep emotions in him?

He sits on the stool at her bureau again and explores her writings. There is an incomplete letter written to Elizabeth.

"My Dearest Elizabeth," it says in big unfocused letters. Henry touches the paper and lets his fingers slide over the writing. There is so much love in it.

Next to it lies a paper with the word "Utopia" written on it with a detailed explanation of how to create a new model of society. His attention is drawn to the words "Queen Anne." Henry smiles. He has known this all along. Her ambitions were clear from the start. She was always intoxicated by power despite her reformist ideals. She always denied this to be the case, but he knew her better than she did herself. Henry scoffs at the word 'Democracy" written under it. He stares at the words "Empowerment of Women." It is an alien concept.

After he puts the papers back, he opens the bureau's top drawer. It is empty. That is odd. He opens the second drawer, and nothing is in there either, but when he opens the bottom drawer, he finds a stack of letters. They are bundled together with a red ribbon. Henry unties it. Immediately, he recognises the letters. His heart is racing. These are letters he wrote to her, love letters.

"She kept them," he says. This is astonishing. He picks one at random and starts reading. "I've put myself into great agony, not knowing how to interpret your letters to me, not knowing how to interpret them, whether to my disadvantage, as you show in some places, or to my advantage, as I understand them in some others…"

Reading his own words out loud brings it all back to him. His devotion, lust and deep love for her. The torture of Anne's ambiguity toward him. Did she love him too, or did she not?

The letters vindicate him as the one who deeply loved her. There were no other motives than true love on his side. Nothing else mattered to him. This can never be disputed.

It makes him sad to think back on how it all turned out. Was Catherine right to claim that his guilt caused his and their demise? Catherine died in early January 1536. Two weeks later, Henry was unhorsed in a tournament and was knocked unconscious. When she received the news, Anne miscarried a baby boy, and four months later, Anne was arrested and executed. Did Catherine curse them?

He hates to think this way and even questions his own sanity, but it must be true. Horrific but undeniable.

Henry reads more fragments from the letters. He knows he is not a great writer. He never was. It was not one of his talents. Aside from certain poems and lyrics, he was the author of merely one book, *Defence of the Seven Sacraments*, written after Martin Luther's attack on indulgences. Ironically, in it, he defends the pope and the

Roman Catholic hierarchy and rituals. Henry was furious that an ordinary monk had dared to attack those who held positions of authority in the Church.

The paradox is that a decade later, he would challenge the pope himself, but this does not bother him. We all hold beliefs and change them, don't we? But what about these letters? Who was this person that wrote these passionate pleas?

It is the flames of passion in them that capture his attention. What was the true nature of these feelings? Was it love or merely lust, or maybe even something greater? A hope and a vision for a complete union? A true love? Or the foolish blabbering of a middle-aged man looking to recover his youth?

"Burn them," a voice behind him whispers, but when he turns around, no one is there. That is strange. He heard the voice clearly. Henry gets up, walks around the room, and even steps out into the hallway, but no one is there.

Burn them? Henry returns to the desk again and holds up one of the letters.

"My mistress and friend, my heart and I surrender ourselves into your hands, beseeching you to hold us commended to your favour and that by absence your affection to us may not be lessened: for it were a great pity to increase our pain, of which absence produces enough and more than I could ever have thought could be felt, reminding us of a point in astronomy which is this: the longer the days are, the more distant is the sun, and nevertheless the hotter; so is it with our love, for by absence we are kept a distance from one another, and yet it retains its fervour, at least on my side."

The writing does not provoke a sentimental feeling in him. The letters are not a rediscovery of a time when everything was innocent and pure. He questions his own words and wonders where these strong emotions came from. What desire or need lies behind them? What is the nature of its true sentiment?

"Burn them." Startled, he stands up again and looks around the room.

"If someone is here, show yourself to me," Henry says. Nothing happens.

Well then, he will burn them, indeed. It may be better to erase these words and lay this tragic love to rest.

He picks them up and squats in front of the fire blazing in the hearth. He holds the first letter to the flames. It ignites immediately, and he lets go of it, then throws the other letters into the fire. Henry stares into the flames. It feels liberating and good to do this. Afterwards, he decides to join Anne in the chapel.

He finds Anne kneeling at the altar. Her head is bowed and rests on her folded hands on the kneeler. She is engrossed in this with all of her being and unaware of his presence behind her. Her voice is full of anguish as she prays quietly to herself.

Henry feels awkward, as if he is intruding into her private world. Maybe he should go back and leave the chapel. He hesitates for a moment. Something tells him to stay, so he kneels on the floor behind her and starts to pray.

His baritone voice startles Anne. Disturbed, she lifts her head and turns around. There is no warmth or relief in her eyes, only hostility, bitterness and surprise, presumably because he has kneeled on the floor to pray.

She does not say anything; she just quickly finishes her prayer. Then she gets up and goes to leave the chapel.

"Anne, wait," he says, standing up. "I've burnt the letters." Anne gives him a questioning look. "The love letters you kept from me. The ones I found in one of the drawers of your bureau," he explains. He is surprised when she starts to laugh harshly.

"There are no letters here from you. Where do you think you are? Hever Castle?"

Her sarcasm hurts his feelings, but he decides not to show it. He is determined to make amends with her.

"They were there. All of them. Bundled together with a red ribbon."

Anne gives this some thought. "Why did you burn them?" she asks after a while.

"I want things to be different between us. I know I've been wrong." Anne starts to laugh again as if what he just shared with her is hilarious.

"Why do you do this?" he asked. "Every time I try to apologise, you ridicule me and my intentions."

Anne gives him a long, hard look. She is about to speak when a massive rumbling causes the floor to tremble. Chalk falls from the walls and the ceiling. Water flows down one of the walls, and a door bursts open in the corner of the chapel.

It does not last long.

Anne looks around the room. The chalk has covered all the furnishings. In the corner of the chapel, Henry notices a door.

"What's behind this door?" he asks, standing in front of it.

Anne removes some of the chalk and looks at the ceiling before she turns to him. "There are so many doors and hallways in this building. This is one I've not opened before. They all lead to nowhere."

Henry pushes the door open. The room behind it is in total darkness.

CHAPTER THIRTY-FOUR
BEHIND CLOSED DOORS

"I'LL NEED some light in here," he says, then fetches the candelabra from behind him.

The door leads into a long, deserted hallway. Within it, there are even more doors. They are all closed except for one. Henry walks over to it and peeks inside.

The room is intimate and small. It is empty like the rest of the house, and the windows are boarded up from the outside. Adjacent to it and connected to it through a doorway is another room.

The second room has a very different layout, which surprises him. A magnificent world has been created in the centre of it on an elevated platform covering most of the interior. It looks like a theatre set, and resembles one of the popular *tableaux vivants*. Wax figures stand as actors in the scene. At the front, near the entrance, is a little sign. It reads, "Greenwich Palace, the Chapel of Observant Friars, September 10, 1533."

The scene shows the christening of Elizabeth. The little princess is only three days old. She is carried by her step-great-grandmother, the old Duchess of Norfolk, and a large silver font stands next to them. They hear church bells as Archbishop Thomas Cranmer recites part of the baptism ceremony.

A party of noblemen that includes Anne's brother, George, carries a crimson satin canopy fringed with gold over the infant's head. One nobleman holds a taper of wax while another man bears the salt. A woman carries the chrisom, which is embroidered with pearls and stones. The entire Boleyn family is present, along with other nobility. Red and blue banners cover the walls, and men with trumpets stand in front of them, ready to blow them after the ceremony is complete.

Henry is fascinated by it all. Who made it?

Quietly, Anne enters the room and looks over his shoulder at the scene.

"Did you create all of this?" Henry asks. Anne shakes her head. She is as astonished as he is.

"It looks so real," she whispers.

Neither of them was present at their daughter's christening, Henry because he was devastated it was not a boy, as predicted, and Anne because it was customary for the mother not to attend.

"I spent so much time preparing for it all, but I never saw it," Anne says. She is truly taken aback by its splendour. The still wax replica of her baby affects her the most. It is almost too much for her.

"Look how beautiful she looks," she says, touching the baby's face. Anne has to stop herself from taking Elizabeth out of the duchess's arms.

"She's so precious." Anne examines every detail of the christening and is elated to see her family present. "My dear father," she whispers when she sees him, "and George."

Henry stands in the doorway, ready to explore the other rooms. "There are more rooms," he says, then disappears with the candelabra into the next chamber while Anne stays behind in the room's shadows.

The sign in front of the next tableau reads, "Palace of Whitehall, January 28, 1547," the date of Henry's death.

"Anne!" he cries. "You have to see this. It's unbelievable."

"This is me on my deathbed," he says when Anne enters, then points at the enormous figure inside the bed.

Beside him sits Elizabeth, who is crying, together with Edward, Mary and Catherine Parr. Also present in the room are Denny and Cranmer.

Anne only has eyes for thirteen-year-old Elizabeth. She does not hear Henry talking about how real it all looks, and she has no interest in the other figures. With tears in her eyes, she walks toward the red-haired teenager in the chair and kneels next to her.

"My poor, sweet Elizabeth," she cries as she tries to comfort her daughter.

"She weeps for me," he says. He expected Anne to take more of an interest in him lying there, but her daughter's presence so absorbs her that she does not hear him. Elizabeth is blossoming into a beauty.

"She's lovely. She's the most beautiful young woman I've ever seen," she says, fondly stroking Elizabeth's long silky hair.

Henry observes how she is with Elizabeth, how she touches her and even presses the wax figure against herself. It makes him quiet and reflective. It is an intimate moment for them both.

Anne looks up at him. "I wish I could talk to her," she says, smiling sadly.

"I'm sure she'd have loved that," he says.

"Do you think so?"

"Of course."

The sign on the next room reads, "Chelsea Manor, May 1548." The scene is set in a bedroom, but it seems odd. Elizabeth, not much older than in the previous room, is lying on a bed. She has a black dress on and is lying on her back. Scandalously, a man in his late thirties, Thomas Seymour, is lying beside her on the bed and appears to be touching her inappropriately.

The woman, who is most likely Seymour's wife, Catherine Parr, stands in the doorway and looks horrified as she observes the scene. On the wall, there is a large painting. It shows the coronation of Edward VI.

"I'm not sure you want to see this. I certainly don't approve of it," Henry says to Anne, who is about to enter the room. Determined to understand what is happening, she walks straight up to the bed.

"Thomas Seymour?" She looks at Henry for an explanation.

"He was good company, and I favoured him, as he was Edward's uncle," Henry says as he stands in front of the painting. "Look at Edward here in the painting."

Anne does not have any interest in it.

"It's Edward's coronation." Henry is pleased to see Edward being crowned king,

"What's Seymour doing on the bed with Elizabeth?" Anne asks. Henry turns around and is unsettled and agitated by the scene as well.

"I think this is all a big misunderstanding," he says to keep them both calm. Clearly, nothing good would come of this.

Anne walks over to Catherine Parr and is surprised to see her own jewellery adorning her neck. "I know this necklace. I wore it myself." She shakes her head in disbelief. "How many wives were there after me? Did you give away all of my possessions to them?" she asks, her voice full of disappointment.

"There was Jane Seymour, Edward's mother," Henry says, but he is immediately interrupted.

"Stop!" Anne cries. "I don't need to know. All I care about is Elizabeth, and I don't understand what's happening here. Is this some future vision?"

"I hope not," Henry says, "but it appears to be." It concerns him. Now he's afraid to enter the next room, but Anne is already walking toward it.

"Tower of London, March 18, 1554," the sign reads.

Anne stands quietly in the room. Elizabeth, now twenty years old, sits behind a desk. It is clear that although the Tower is a royal palace, Elizabeth is not a visitor; she is being kept prisoner by her elder sister, Mary.

On the wall, a painting depicts the coronation of Mary. Henry studies the painting with interest and notices that Elizabeth is also in the painting. But what happened to Edward?

"Nothing changes. She is clearly her father's daughter," Anne says, pointing to the painting of Mary. She is bitter and angry, her eyes blazing with fury.

"Are you sure you want to see the next room?" Henry asks, but it is too late. Anne has already entered it.

CHAPTER THIRTY-FIVE
ASCENSION

THE SIGN on this door reads, "Westminster Abbey, November 17, 1558. The coronation of Queen Elizabeth."

In the centre of the room sits Elizabeth in her coronation robes, patterned with Tudor roses and trimmed with ermine. On her head is an ornate crown, and she carries the orb and sceptre that Henry used at his coronation. In the background, they hear the congregation of the abbey hail their new queen.

Anne puts her hands in front of her mouth and lets out a shriek of excitement. With tears in her eyes, she walks over to Elizabeth and curtsies in front of her. "Hail Your Majesty, Queen Elizabeth … I can't say how proud and happy I am," she says when she turns to Henry. "She looks phenomenal."

He agrees with her, but at the same time, he feels very unsettled by everything he has seen. What about the others? What about Mary and Edward?

"If this is the future of my little girl…" Anne stops, overwhelmed with emotion. "Then all is well."

There is one more room.

"I'm not sure if this will bring good news, but I need to know," Anne says. She opens the door to the sound of cannon fire and enters the room.

A sign says, "The defeat of the Spanish Armada, 1588."

In the centre of the room, Elizabeth stands upright with confidence and authority as a timeless queen in a lavish silver satin and black velvet dress ornately decorated with gemstones. Her striking red hair is pinned up, styled with curls, and embellished with an abundance of pearls. The starched lace of her ruff encircles her pale and ageless face and makes her stand out as a larger-than-life figure.

Elizabeth almost looks like a deity, majestic and serene. Her right hand rests on a globe on a table covered with green silk cloth. The part of the globe facing them shows the territory of the New World, and Elizabeth's hand seems to suggest she is in charge of it.

Next to her, on the right, is a large crown, and behind her are paintings of the victorious English fleet on one side and the defeated and destroyed Spanish Armada on the other.

Henry and Anne are both stunned by Elizabeth's presence. In silence, they stare at their daughter, unable to comprehend the monarch she will become. It is clear that during her reign, England will prosper. It will become great.

Anne is the first to speak. "I could never have dreamt this for Elizabeth. You can tell from everything she's a supreme queen. Look at her face and her eyes. She looks so beautiful, so gentle and wise, and yet so strong and unafraid."

"She's truly a Tudor queen," he says, pointing to the Tudor roses embroidered on her dress.

"She's a true Reformer who defeated a Catholic invasion," Anne says.

"She wants to rule the world with an English fleet," Henry observes.

"But she's not married," Anne points out as she touches Elizabeth's hands. Elizabeth is wearing only one ring. Diamonds on the ring show the letter "E" for "Elizabeth" and the letter "R" for "Regina" in blue enamel.

There is something peculiar. In her left hand, Elizabeth is holding a small black box. It looks like she wants to offer someone a gift. Anne spots it too.

She hesitates, then takes the box out of Elizabeth's hand and opens it.

"It's a replica of the ring she's wearing," Anne says, not understanding its significance. "Wait a moment. It's a locket ring." Anne struggles to open it, but then the ring's secret compartment falls open, revealing painted miniature reliefs of Elizabeth and

Anne facing each other.

Anne does not say anything. She just stares at the ring, deeply touched by it all. She kisses it gently and holds it to her heart. Trembling, she tries the ring on. It fits perfectly. She looks at Elizabeth, takes a step back, bows in reverence, and then kisses her daughter's hands.

What happens next is astonishing. The wax figure starts to change. It becomes human with soft, warm hands, a smiling face and open, loving eyes. Light surrounds Elizabeth, and a profound love radiates from her.

Henry observes this miracle and witnesses how these two women, mother and daughter, embrace as if they are both alive. "My beautiful daughter," Anne says, sobbing with joy.

Everything happens quickly. Strong emotions surround these two women, and instead of words, beautiful colours, including silver and gold, emerge from their mouths and engulf them. Their souls fuse as one. A profound exchange occurs, revealing all the details of Elizabeth's life to Anne's spirit, and to her alone.

Henry can see that Anne knows everything. She does not need Utopia anymore. She does not want to become a queen herself any longer. She has seen the golden age that her daughter's reign will bring to England. It's more than she could ever have wished for. Now, all she wants is to return home to be with her dearest father and mother, and siblings.

Henry can see how happy and at peace Anne is, and in the final moments, she turns to Henry and smiles. "I'm finally free," she says to him. "Go in peace."

The wings of an archangel wrap around her body. Her black gown is transformed into a white robe, and her hair hangs down over her shoulders. She looks serene and beautiful.

The angel then emits a light so bright that Henry must cover his eyes with his arms.

A stairway into the heavens appears, and many more angels line up along each side and blow trumpets to welcome the new arrival.

Anne smiles and laughs as she ascends the stairway, where she is greeted by the heavenly realms and is recognised as the incredible soul that she is.

The vision is so wonderful to behold that Henry starts to cry. He realises that he has not protected or honoured her spirit, but violated it. A deep regret fills his entire being. He falls to his knees, and prays with a contrite heart. "Have mercy on me, God. Forgive me."

CHAPTER THIRTY-SIX
THE FAMILY LEGACY

EVERYTHING IS GONE: Anne, Elizabeth, the scene about the defeat of the Spanish Armada, everything. Henry stands alone in an empty room.

Without it, everything feels cold and lifeless. He hurries to the adjacent room, hoping to find Anne or anything, but there are no traces of the tableau there either. Neither is there in the other rooms. Even the chapel that Anne had devoted to Elizabeth has been stripped bare.

With the candelabra in his hand, he searches for any signs or tokens that belong to Anne, or a hint of the chapel that existed just moments ago, but there is nothing, only dust and pieces of chalk on the floor. It is not as if the altar and the furniture have been removed; it looks as if they were never there in the first place.

How can this be? He runs to the drawing room. Surely, he will find something there that belongs to her, but when he enters, it is another deserted and abandoned room.

For a moment, he wonders if he got lost, opened the wrong door, or walked through the wrong hallway. The manor is a bit of a labyrinth, and he may have become confused.

With quick steps, he returns to where he thought the chapel was and to the rooms with the *tableaux vivants*. But they all look the same.

Not someone to give up easily, he walks back and forth between rooms and hallways in disbelief until he suddenly has an idea. He hurries back to what once was Anne's drawing room.

The room is without furniture or decoration, like all the others, but when he looks for the fireplace, he is excited to see it is still there. He squats in front of the hearth and pokes around in the ashes, looking for fragments of burnt paper.

Indeed, after a while, he finds a fragment of yellow and brown paper in the corner behind some charred wood. He holds it to the candlelight. "*Votre loyal serviteur et ami,*" it says. "Your loyal servant and friend." This tiny fragment from one of his letters proves that he is not going mad. But what else does it prove? Profound feelings of disorientation and isolation fill him.

He tries to remember the drawing room as it was before. He sits with his back against the wall and imagines all the time that Anne must have been alone in this room.

Her absence leaves a painful void. Even when she was obstinate and crusading for her obsessions, she was still radiant. She was always that way. So full of enthusiasm and passion, full of anger and fire too. She would scorch the earth if she had to.

He misses her and regrets everything. It still feels unfinished and incomplete, but maybe that is the tragedy of life, the cross he must bear.

During his life, he did not feel this unique connection with anyone else. No other woman or man stoked this kind of fire or had this kind of hold over him.

After Anne's death on the scaffold, he forbade Elizabeth or anyone else to mention her name. Maybe this was to hide the guilt of what he had done.

Princess Elizabeth was, in the end, his daughter and no one else's. She had no mother, at least not a mother she could ever mention or speak of publicly.

With Anne, the Boleyns, or what was left of them, vanished from public life too. After Sir Thomas' death, Henry took possession of Hever Castle and gave it away as a divorce gift to Anne of Cleves. A mistake he bitterly regrets. With her father's death and Hever Castle given to his ex-wife, he succeeded in erasing Anne's presence. There was no trace left of her, just like now.

It is true that despite Anne's strength, he always knew she was vulnerable, even fragile. She put on a brave face. And while he sits in this room, he imagines her at court again and can hear her laughter. She was always surrounded by admiring men or with her friends or close family members, chatting, gossiping and expressing her sometimes provocative opinions.

She would occasionally stir things up for no reason, but most of the time, she was attentive to whoever crossed her path. She was a good listener and showed a genuine interest in those who confided in her and the topics they brought to her attention.

Sometimes she was quiet, like a shy and dreamy little girl who was lost in her own world and would sit in a corner all by herself. She was all that and so much more. He loved her; he knows that. He can no longer deny it.

Henry reflects on what he witnessed in the tableaux with the wax figures. Curious to better understand the chain of events as they were presented, he tries to piece it all together. His memory is good, and he recalls every detail, like the paintings that depicted Edward and Mary's coronations.

He realises that all his children will be king or queen at some point. This satisfies him, even though he regrets the limited time that Edward and Mary will have.

He thinks about Edward, who was always polite to him and made an effort to impress him. The boy was studious and had a good temperament. According to some reports, Edward had a cruel and unpleasant streak when dealing with animals. He could not imagine it to be true. He recognises that boys are boys, but his son would never treat an animal in a sadistic way, would he?

But what about Mary?

He sighs deeply. She never forgave him for what happened to her mother. He would always see it in her eyes. Her mother filled her mind and heart with hatred for him. In the end, Mary would sacrifice her own happiness and life for it. At least, this is how he sees it. Catherine was selfish by demanding her daughter's loyalty and plotting against him.

Henry and Anne's legacy will be Elizabeth's triumph as the queen who defeated the Spanish Armada and the ruler of the New World to come. This is a success he would have loved to have achieved himself. It will change everything in Europe and on the seas around the world. It is astonishing that his little girl will manage to do such a thing. He smiles. A woman and not a man.

Who would have thought?

Reflecting on these future events makes him happy initially, but the feeling does not last long. His daughter's projected future makes his role and position in history less unique and important. How will he be represented? Will Cromwell be proved right? What he spoke of in the dungeon frightens him. It would be a justice of sorts for those he has wronged.

"'Generations come, and generations go,'" he says quietly, "but the earth remains forever. The sun rises, and the sun sets." He quotes the entire verse from Ecclesiastes 1 and ends with, "'What has been will be again, and what has been done will be done again; there is nothing new under the sun. There is no remembrance of those who came before, and yet to come will not be remembered by those who follow after.'"

The storm outside has passed. There's not a single sound in the building. No creaky wooden panels, dripping water or the sound of the wind blowing through the chimneys and dusty hallways - nothing. He hates being all by himself. What happens now?

In the semi-darkness of the room, he thinks back to when he was lying on his deathbed in Whitehall. It comforts him to imagine himself back in the palace, surrounded by those who attend him and care for him.

Throughout his life, there was always an army of people at court to keep him occupied and amused. There were dramas and intrigue, plots and counterplots, and decisions to be made. Not one moment seemed idle; instead, there was a constant barrage of events or things to do. They consumed most of his time—the hunts, the balls, the music, the flirtations and the infatuations, the visits to the shipyards, the meetings with his privy chamber. "Live as if there is no tomorrow" was his motto. But what about now?

One builds things, works hard, fights and loves. One disagrees about the law, the Bible and how one should behave. One takes up all sorts of projects and responsibilities, yet never thinks about death and how short life is. People think they will live forever, or at least another decade or another year or two or maybe even three, until it finally stops, and then they take their last breath.

Was Henry's life worth it? Was it worth living? Did he find true love? Does he now finally understand what it was all about? Is there truly a connection and a faith that goes beyond his own limitations and the physical realm we call life? And will he indeed be reunited with his maker?

Or are some souls destined to remain behind in an empty hallway, lost in an empty palace? Why did the angels come for Anne and Catherine but not him?

"It will change," he says, his voice reverberating through the empty room. "Surely someone will come and knock on the door. Someone will come to end this..."

CHAPTER THIRTY-SEVEN
TRINITY

NOTHING STAYS THE SAME FOREVER. It would be torture. The story of life and the universe itself is that everything changes due to what has come before. Things can be a thousand or a million times the same, but a subtle difference or aberration can lead to a new and unexpected formation.

Sometimes this change comes as a sudden, irreversible rupture. It brings havoc and revolution, and structures that stood firm for a long time collapse and are replaced with new frontiers and revelations. This is all God's breath multiplying and diversifying everything without end.

Even now, after sitting in a dark, quiet corner of the room in this deserted building with its empty rooms, Henry realises that change has also come for him. He feels it. It has come as a shadow, almost like a secret that has entered his world. A new decor has been created; a novel space in which to exist has been designed and realised. Henry stretches and raises himself from his dark little corner, readying himself to explore it.

The room, which lies hidden in the dark, is no longer empty. It is filled with furniture, rugs, tapestries and paintings. He smiles.

As Henry investigates the room, he finds everything in it looks monumental. The fireplace is over eight feet tall, and the pillars with the sculptures that are part of the mantel, supporting the upper shelf, have formidable proportions and project immense power and wealth. The size and grandeur of the room feel familiar to him. It feels like home.

The room isn't a replica of one of the rooms in Whitehall, Hampton Court, Greenwich or any other of his palaces. It is unique.

Curious, he walks around with the candelabra and holds it up to get a better view of the paintings and huge tapestries that cover the walls.

One of the tapestries shows Zacchaeus climbing a sycamore tree to get a glimpse of Jesus coming his way. The description of the scene is woven into it. The quality of the tapestry is similar to the Flemish and Italian tapestries that Henry is familiar with. Its golden and silver threads shimmer in the candlelight. In the semi-darkness of the room, they are vibrant and sparkle magically.

Zacchaeus was a wealthy tax collector who worked for the Romans. Like all men of his profession, he was loathed by most, and with good reason. He had lived a deceitful life dominated by greed, and many suffered because of his actions.

When Jesus saw Zacchaeus in the tree, He told him to come down immediately and invited Himself to his house.

The idea that Jesus would visit a sinner like Zacchaeus did not go down well with his followers, but Zacchaeus stood and said, "Look, Lord! Here and now, I give half of my possessions to the poor, and if I have cheated anybody out of anything, I will pay back four times the amount." Jesus welcomed the man's salvation and embraced him as a son of Abraham.

Henry stares at the various scenes depicted in the tapestry. It is a lesson he failed to learn as king, and he knows it. Zacchaeus was eager to see Jesus, setting his pride aside to do so. He accepted Jesus's call and invitation and allowed himself to be changed. Maybe it's not too late for Henry to do the same.

The manor has been transformed into a palace, and it appears he is no longer alone. From the hallway along the main corridor, he hears muffled voices, shrieks of laughter and footsteps. This rouses Henry's curiosity. Excitedly, he leaves the room.

The long, dark hallway next to the room is decorated with large paintings of all the past English kings and queens, including his parents. This intrigues and pleases Henry. He studies each one for a moment before moving toward the main hall, from the source of the light and voices.

The hall has undergone a metamorphosis, and a magnificent dance is underway. There is music, and candles are burning everywhere. The hall is filled with guests, but nobody seems to notice Henry's entrance or show any interest in his presence. What is also striking is that all the men and women are masked. They are dressed in fine clothes and look elegant, talking with each other as they dance and laugh. Somehow it feels as if they are not part of his reality, but are in a world of their own.

One person stands out. He is all alone on the other side of the hall. When Henry looks at him, the masked young man nods and walks over to him. A rush of excitement comes over Henry. Who is this young man?

When the stranger is standing face to face with Henry, he removes his mask. Henry smiles.

"It's you," Henry says, pleased to see his son, the Duke of Cornwall.

"We meet again," the young duke says, smiling warmly.

"Who are all these people?" Henry asks.

"I have no idea," Young Henry says. "It doesn't matter anyway."

"I find that hard to believe." Henry looks around the room. "The architecture is impressive. It looks like something I could've designed myself." Henry examines the wooden arches supporting the roof and the oversized tapestries on the walls. "I'm pleased to see more tapestries here as well."

"You love tapestries, don't you?"

"Love them?" Henry chuckles. "I was obsessed with them."

"What's the story on this one?" Henry asks as he steps toward one of the tapestries on the wall behind him to get a better look. Young Henry is about to tell him, but Henry holds up his hand to stop him. "Hold on, let me find it out for myself." He studies the tapestry. No title is woven into it, but it should not be difficult to figure out the scene.

"A king who is ready for battle," he says, pointing at the king in the tapestry who is wearing a full suit of armour. "A king anointed by God." Henry falls quiet. In another segment, a naked woman is depicted taking a bath. The same king is also in this segment, spying on her from his balcony. Henry's face clouds over. Sadness seems to overtake him.

"King David and Bathsheba," he says. "Did you come here to teach me another lesson?"

Young Henry shakes his head. "I didn't put it here."

"If not you, then who?" Henry asks.

"God loved David more than any other king," Young Henry says. Henry knows this is true. He studied David's kingship closely.

"Yet, he was flawed and a sinner," Henry says.

David committed adultery with Bathsheba and murdered her husband, Uriah. As a punishment, their first child, a son, died right after birth. It makes Henry quiet and reflective for a moment.

"Anne suffered a great injustice," he says, looking at the lad.

"She wasn't the only one hurt by your actions." Young Henry speaks without strong emotion or even a hint of an accusation, but still, Henry is taken aback by his observation, and is hurt by it. The young lad has never criticised him before.

"Your mother was a stubborn and difficult woman. I see she has turned you against me," he says on impulse, then immediately regrets it. This is no longer the time to rake over the past. Not with his son.

As if everyone in the hall has heard his remark, the music stops, as does the dancing. All those present turn toward Henry and stare at him in silent judgment.

Young Henry takes a few steps back, then lets out a shriek of pain. He brings his hand to his heart. The young lad is clearly in distress.

"What's wrong?" Henry asks in alarm. His son looks pale and uncomfortable. Henry doesn't know what to do. "Did I do this to you? Was it what I just said about your mother?"

The duke needs a moment to recover. Henry feels tempted to explain himself and to tell him how difficult it was to live with Catherine, but he holds back, realising it may hurt the boy even more. Instead, he prays silently in the hope that God will spare his son and, in exchange, do with Henry what He will.

It is an awkward situation. Henry turns to the guests, who stare at them in silence. It makes him very uncomfortable.

"What are you looking at? Go, and leave us alone!" he shouts, but nobody moves.

Young Henry is still squirming in pain. Henry never intended to hurt the boy. "Is there anything I can do to help? Anything?"

The duke tries to produce a smile, but it looks more like a grimace. "Are you still angry with my mother? Are you angry with me?"

Henry waits before he responds. All the anger and frustration that he felt for years after Catherine failed to produce a male heir, and the bitter divorce that followed, resurface in him like an old enemy. He sees how they ruined his once happy marriage to Catherine and set him on a path of destruction. The pain only subsided a little when Edward was born.

He could lie to the boy. Then again, why not tell the truth? Nothing good ever comes from a lie. That much he learnt from his dealings with Anne.

"I loved your mother once. But we both made choices and mistakes. Over time things changed between us. Our love grew cold. I betrayed her and hurt her. That is a burden I must carry alone and atone for. But I never wished to hurt you. At the time, I was seeking a son. I was seeking you. I didn't know it then, but seeing you now, my first begotten son... I deeply mourned your loss. It changed me forever." Beginning to weep, Henry reaches for his son's hand.

This has a remarkable effect on Young Henry. All at once he recovers his posture, and whatever pain was there leaves him. He seems at ease again. The lad reaches out to touch his father's hand. Then they embrace each other, and for the first time, Henry feels at peace.

Distracted, Henry looks around at the guests, but they suddenly melt like ice left out in the sun. Bit by bit, they disappear until no one is left.

"They weren't real, were they?"

Young Henry looks innocent and yet shows wisdom far beyond his years. He nods and smiles. "Nothing in Limbo is real," he says. "Everything is an illusion."

After he says this, the hall undergoes another transformation. A strong light breaks through the windows that had been boarded up and covered with heavy sumptuous crimson curtains.

This pleases Young Henry. His father, on the other hand, is not so certain and is frightened by the change. The light suddenly dims. "Is this a trap?" he asks. "What's happening?"

"You are too fearful and pessimistic," his son says, his voice full of concern. "You do not trust the power of love. It's the greatest gift God created. Have faith in it. If you fear love, the darkness will imprison you in your fear and pride."

Henry doesn't say anything, but is disappointed by his son's remark. A part of him wishes to retaliate in anger and to defend himself. The effect on the lad is immediate and profound. He withdraws from Henry further and tries to suppress his anguish and concern.

It is not only Henry's son who is affected. The bright light that wants to come in from outside dims even further, as if a dark cloud has obscured the sun.

Then Henry observes something remarkable in the young man's face. In it, Henry sees his own features mirrored back. It is not merely the red hair and the clear blue eyes, the fine, straight nose, the large forehead and strong jaw. Something in his son's eyes reminds him of the innocence that he lost as a child when his mother died.

"Why did you come back to help me?" he asks, his voice full of warmth. He looks at his son and is happy to be close to him.

"It's time," Young Henry says, a sudden sense of urgency in his voice. "The window to transition away from Limbo is closing, and it will get much harder for you to cross over. You must choose now, without delay."

"I've sinned more than David. I've hurt your mother and even denied your legitimacy. I've killed those I once loved and condemned many to die without just cause, but now when I look into your eyes, I see my own reflection and that of your mother, my parents and their ancestors. They're all here watching me now. How could I not love you? My son. Forgive me. Allow me to receive your love. You once offered it to me, and I was a fool to refuse you," he says with heartfelt emotion.

It is as if the sun has come out again. The light of its warm healing rays floods the hall. The light surrounding them is bright and intensifies even further.

"God loved King David, but David exploited his power as a king," Henry says. "When he realised this, he repented without reservation. I, too, repent and will do whatever God deems necessary. Please come here, my son."

Young Henry stands in front of him. Their faces are close, and in this brief, magical moment, a powerful love flows out from the duke into Henry. It is a love so pure and beautiful that it brings tears of joy to Henry's eyes and an inner peace he's never known.

In his son, Henry sees the complete journey of his soul. The lifetimes he has lived both long ago and those he has yet to live. He experiences his mother's love again, a love that was cruelly taken from him as a child, and the Light of all that is. It embraces Henry without judgment, heals him, and, like the loving father in the parable of the prodigal son, welcomes him home.

EPILOGUE

IT IS 4 am in Richmond Palace. The royal bedchamber is intimate and sparsely lit. A 69-year-old Queen Elizabeth sits wide awake in the plush purple velvet armchair beside the boat-shaped bed. Her breathing is shallow and hastened.

Without one of her imposing wigs, her face appears even more striking in the dark. Her freckled skin, washed with asses' milk and rose water, is blotchy and wrinkled, but her eyes are as penetrating and fiery as in daylight.

Her companion, one of the ladies of the bedchamber, watches her with concern and is about to ask her mistress if there is anything she needs.

"I don't believe it!" she gasps. "It was her!"

Her lady-in-waiting stares at her, perplexed.

Elizabeth, in her nightdress, stands up as if she is about to take action, only to fall back into the chair again.

Her hard and combative demeanour softens, and a gentle vulnerability appears in her eyes.

"She smiled at me. Then she held me close," Elizabeth says, and her face lights up. "I instantly knew it was her. There was no doubt."

"Who, Your Grace?"

Elizabeth does not answer her. Instead, she remembers her dream: the warmth and love in the woman's eyes.

She looks down at the locket ring on her finger. Its band is set with rubies. Six white diamonds create the letter 'E', which covers the letter 'R'. An impressive pearl is set next to it. The ring is her most treasured possession, her secret.

Elizabeth opens the locket and smiles at the two miniatures delicately painted inside. She closes the locket, lifts her hand and kisses the ring gently.

"Some dreams, like nightmares, remind us of our guilt and shortcomings," she says. "They are there to teach us a lesson and guide us, but this was different. It was a message from the other side. A whisper of love."

"Who appeared in Your Majesty's dream?"

Elizabeth shakes her head. She will not answer that question. Not even here in the privacy of her own bedchamber. She has said too much already.

"Don't pressure me to share my innermost thoughts with you," Elizabeth lashes out and looks at the young woman displeased.

The lady-in-waiting apologises profusely, but Elizabeth pays her no heed.

Why did the woman appear to her now after all these years? She ponders on this for a while.

In the past, she would have asked John Dee, her astrologer, for his assessment of the dream. She could confide in him, and he would have clarified it.

She trembles and tears well up in her eyes. This was not an ordinary dream. It felt so incredibly real, as real as life itself. Most of all, it was monumental. It had filled her entire being with an unconditional love she had never known but had often fantasised about as a child—her mother's love.

She stares into the darkness of her bedchamber.

In her mind, fragments of her life present themselves as part of a bigger picture. Among them are her coronation and her glorious defeat of the Spanish Armada. The victory established her greatness, and she did it all without being beholden to a man in marriage.

She is her father's daughter. She is strong-willed, shrewd, intelligent, determined and powerful, as any man that has ruled before her. But she also embodies her mother's independent spirit, passionate nature and love of beauty and justice.

There is another realisation. Elizabeth R, the glorious *Faerie Queene*, is the pinnacle of the Tudor dynasty. Its legacy will have an impact for generations. This thought pleases her.

Elizabeth leans back in the chair, satisfied that both her mother and father would be proud of their little girl, especially her mama. "May you rest in peace," she whispers.

12 BOOK CLUB
QUESTIONS

1   Why would you recommend this book to someone? What kind of reader would most enjoy this book?

2   Did you find the author's writing style easy to read or hard to read? Why? How long did it take you to get into the book?

3   Who was your favourite character? What character did you identify with the most? Were there any characters that you disliked? Why?

4   Did any part of this book strike a particular emotion in you? Which part and what emotion did the book make you feel?

5   What surprised you the most about the book?

6   Was there any part of the plot or aspects of the characters that frustrated or upset you? If so, why?

7   How thought-provoking did you find the book? Did the book change your opinion about anything, or did you learn something new from it? If so, what?

8   Did you highlight or bookmark any passages from the book? Do you have a favourite quote or quotes? If so, share which and why?

9   From your point of view, what were the central themes of the book? How well do you think the author did at exploring them?

10   Compare this book to others you have read covering the same or similar themes. How are they the same or different?

11   How would you adapt this book into a movie? Who would you cast in the leading roles?

12   Rate this book on a scale of 1 to 10, with 10 being the highest. Why did you give the book the rating you did? Did any part of this book club discussion change your rating from what it would have been directly after finishing the book?

Jan Hendrik Verstraten studied film in New York and sold his first film to PBS. He ran successful companies in pottery and design. His foray into writing began when he moved to London, with a play he took to the Edinburgh Fringe Festival. Several screenplays followed and in 2015, he wrote and directed the short film titled *I am Henry* about Henry VIII, Anne Boleyn and Catherine of Aragon.

The film was co-produced by **Massimo Barbato** and marked the start of their creative partnership. They both love history and became fascinated by this tragic royal love triangle. *I am Henry* received excellent reviews from historians, Tudor lovers and The Telegraph critic Patrick Smith. It was shown at festivals worldwide, won many awards and remains a popular short film on Amazon Prime.

Today, Jan Hendrik and Massimo run the arthouse New Renaissance Film Festival, which they founded in 2016. During lockdown, inspired by the success of *I am Henry*, Massimo suggested to start working together on a book based on the film. They both felt that it was important to stay true to historical fact as much as possible, although the novel is a fictional and personal interpretation. Massimo had previously written a book about the cultural impact of artificial intelligence and had many articles published in various magazines. He hopes to work on many more books with Jan Hendrik. With postgraduate degrees in law, marketing and theology, Massimo also tutors university students. The authors live in London.

Historical Fiction

I Am Henry - **Jan Hendrik Verstraten & Massimo Barbato**
The Sebastian Foxley Series - **Toni Mount**
The Death Collector - **Toni Mount**

Historical Colouring Books

The Mary, Queen of Scots Colouring Book - **Roland Hui**
The Life of Anne Boleyn Colouring Book - **Claire Ridgway**
The Wars of the Roses Colouring Book - **Debra Bayani**
The Tudor Colouring Book - **Ainhoa Modenes**

Non Fiction History

Tudor Places of Great Britain - **Claire Ridgway**
Illustrated Kings and Queens of England - **Claire Ridgway**
A History of the English Monarchy - **Gareth Russell**
The Fall of Anne Boleyn - **Claire Ridgway**
George Boleyn - **Ridgway & Cherry**
The Anne Boleyn Collection I, II & III - **Claire Ridgway**
Jasper Tudor - **Debra Bayani**
The Turbulent Crown - **Roland Hui**
Two Gentleman Poets at the Court of Henry VIII - **Edmond Bapst**

PLEASE LEAVE A REVIEW

If you enjoyed this book, *please*
leave a review at the book seller
where you purchased it. There is
no better way to thank the author
and it really does make a huge
difference!
Thank you in advance.

Printed in Great Britain
by Amazon

31556022R00110